Praise for *Weaned Seals and Snowy Summits*

"I can't think of a better time for *Weaned Seals and Snowy Summits: Stories of Passion for Place and Everyday Nature* to appear. Given our current environmental crisis, connection (or reconnection) to the natural world is not just a crucial emotional or spiritual experience, it could well be the key to our survival. Jennifer J. Wilhoit, Ph.D. and Stephen B. Jones, Ph.D. pool their talents to present compelling essays explaining why we need nature every bit as much as nature needs us. These are rich tales of travel and wonder, and each contributes to our understanding of the interdependence of life. This is a first-rate road map to the heart of life."

> – Burt J. Kempner Award-Winning Writer-Producer, Author of *The Five Fierce Tigers of Rosa Martinez*, and Co-Creator of the Rewilding the Human Machine Forum

"Jennifer Wilhoit and Steve Jones have collaborated to create an enchanting, inspiring, and important book. Their voices are strong, clear, informed, and poetic. The result is a conversation, even though they have each written a series of individual essays. Together, they help to bring lessons from nature to life in our everyday lives at a time of urgent need."

> – Cheryl Charles, Ph.D. Co-Founder, President, and CEO Emerita, Children and Nature Network, and Adjunct Faculty and Executive Director, Nature Based Leadership Institute, Antioch University New England

"Through *Weaned Seals and Snowy Summits: Stories of Passion for Place and Everyday Nature*, Wilhoit and Jones surpass commonplace concepts of earth stewardship and connectivity by providing a compelling, passionate, and memorable journey through transcendent prose. From rare personal experiences with baby elephant seals to everyday familiarities with wildflowers and butterflies, readers will delight in this expedition across planet Earth. This is more than a book about biodiversity and observations; it is an intimate invitation to rediscover the enchantment of our natural world. A powerful reminder that whether we are in a forest primeval, in a public park, on a wild beach, or in our own back yard, every moment in nature is a once upon a time moment."

– Renee Simmons Raney Environmental Educator and Author

"Richly descriptive passages and philosophical musings come together in this powerful narrative on nature. Jennifer Wilhoit and Steve Jones share their personal and professional encounters with the great outdoors in language that is scientifically grounded but highly accessible and engaging. Life, death, diversity, transitions, ambiguity, and passion all get their due in this retrospective of first-hand encounters with nature in all its glory."

– Kristin Tichenor, Ed.D. Senior Vice President Worcester Polytechnic Institute

"The authors' emphasis on the practice of Earth stewardship is an exultation of life on an ancient planet lately overshadowed by the gritty naivete of humankind. Dr. Wilhoit's pithy examination of the ecotone between planet and people is a message of sheer poetry as we hunger for wholeness in that helter-skelter relationship. Wilhoit's and Jones' carefully worded manifesto inspires me with a song of gratitude for nature's wonder-filled complexity."

– H. Bruce Rinker, Ph.D. Ecologist, Educator, Explorer, and Author of A Pearl in the Brain: The Cancer Journey of a Scientist in His Search for the Seat of the Soul

"Drawing from the authors' vast experiences, we are reminded that life isn't about the big adventures. It is about the awareness of the relationships we can have with the natural world if we simply take the time—like with any healthy relationship—to respectfully and responsibly engage. Rich with texture and imagery, Wilhoit and Jones find a way to re-connect us with our own selves and with one other, using the natural world as our template. Through the richness of the authors' ability to draw us into the back yard of our lives, we see how the textures of nature work in relationship with each other and with humans. In *Weaned Seals and Snowy Summits*, we are taken to the place of understanding where we can create an ecotone of our own— that place where humans and nature not only co-exist within one another, but thrive—thereby defining right relationship in a way that is palpable, and most hopefully, probable."

> – Kate Trnka, M.S.Ed. Owner of Sacred Earth Wellness and Sacred Earth Publishing, and Charter for Compassion Environment Sector Lead Ambassador/Global Read Coordinator

"*Weaned Seals and Snowy Summits* is an engaging read flowing from the minds of two lifelong nature-appreciating people. Each author shares about their relationship with the Earth and its multitude of wonders. For example, in one essay Dr. Jones highlights its flora (forest ecology) and in another Dr. Wilhoit focuses on its fauna (elephant seals). Together, they address throughout their book how to think about sustainability of all life on our Earth."

> – James T. McGill, Ph.D. Sr. VP, Finance and Administration, Johns Hopkins University, Retired

"I was happy to hear that Jennifer Wilhoit and Steve Jones have collaborated to produce a book that is aimed at capturing their respective experiences in nature and then motivating readers to find their own ways to capture nature-based experiences wherever they might be located. They succinctly state that anyone can develop a relationship with nature wherever they are, and they reiterate that point in each essay of the book. An ultimate goal of the text is to motivate readers to develop an understanding and appreciation of our relationship to Earth and the imperative to act accordingly. It is the hope of the authors that the book offers guidance and inspiration to motivate readers to make their own connection to Earth and all beings more tangible, more a part of daily life, richer and more dynamic. Readers will be mentally taken on field trips into nature with Wilhoit and Jones, and their observational writing skills will offer lessons that can be used in everyday life."

– Ronald G. Dodson Author, Speaker, Entrepreneur

Other Books by Jennifer J. Wilhoit

Writing on the Landscape (2017)
Weaving a Network (2009)
Common Ground Between Crafts Collectives and Conservation (2008)

Other Books by Stephen B. Jones

Nature-Inspired Learning and Leading (2017)
Nature Based Leadership (2016)

Weaned Seals and Snowy Summits

Stories of Passion for Place and Everyday Nature

Jennifer J. Wilhoit, Ph.D. and Stephen B. Jones, Ph.D.

LifeRich Publishing is a registered trademark of The Reader's Digest Association, Inc.

LifeRich Publishing books may be ordered through booksellers or by contacting:

LifeRich Publishing
1663 Liberty Drive
Bloomington, IN 47403
www.liferichpublishing.com
1 (888) 238-8637

Because of the dynamic nature of the Internet, any web addresses or links contained in this book may have changed since publication and may no longer be valid. The views expressed in this work are solely those of the author and do not necessarily reflect the views of the publisher, and the publisher hereby disclaims any responsibility for them.

ISBN: 978-1-4897-2352-9 (sc)
ISBN: 978-1-4897-2351-2 (hc)
ISBN: 978-1-4897-2353-6 (e)

Library of Congress Control Number: 2019908340

Print information available on the last page.

LifeRich Publishing rev. date: 08/09/2019

Dedication

For Cynthia Lynn Thompson Wilhoit ... vibrant nature-loving artist

and

For Judy Jones ... and the many miles we've shared

Contents

Acknowledgments

Though only two of us put pen to page to write *Weaned Seals and Snowy Summits*, it was a community effort. I so gratefully acknowledge:

Our early readers and blurb writers – through whose eyes we were able to see a broader and deeper vision

Co-author Steve Jones – whose patience, compassion, cooperation, and stories made this book possible

My friends – who bless me in ways they might never imagine, even when I'm hidden away at my writing desk

My younger brother Sean – who makes me laugh more heartily than anyone else on the planet, and who is wise in ways I will never be

My older sisters Melissa and Sheila – whose friendship, support, and love have made this difficult year gloriously more tolerable, and who are always there

My sweetheart – who knows why

The creatures and landscapes of Earth – that sustain, soothe, enlighten, and inspire me …*JJW*

Long-time friends and colleagues Craig Cassarino, Ron Dodson, and Bob Kellison spur me to apply the passion of my beliefs to the service

of Earth stewardship. Ray Silverman guides and informs my journey to understand, appreciate, and apply the spiritual dimension of my lifelong relationship to nature. Dixie Yann, as Fairmont State University Board Chair during my interim presidency, enabled me to experience the most rewarding senior administrative post of my career. They and too many others to name helped position me to transition from fulltime employment into my capstone semi-retirement niche as author, speaker, and champion of nature's wisdom, power, and inspiration. Co-author Jennifer Wilhoit believes in my writing and has improved my craft by leaps and bounds. …*SBJ*

Introduction

Aldo Leopold observed: *There are some who can live without wild things and some who cannot.* I co-authored this book of essays for those who cannot and also for those who might be so persuaded.

We humans now number 7.7 billion. Our Earth is finite; our demand for her resources (e.g., water, minerals, fossil fuels, clean air, wood, tillable land, open space, scenic beauty, and wildness) grows exponentially. My intent for these essays is to spur an awakening to our species' absolute dependence upon our planet. We do not stand apart from nature; we are one with nature.

Isolated and alone, the thriving civilization on Easter Island could not sustain, consuming the Pacific island's precious limited resources beyond a critical threshold. Similarly, we are isolated and alone, so far as we know, on island Earth. Living on a mote of dust in the vast darkness of space, we cannot count on being rescued from elsewhere. Only we can (and must) protect us from ourselves. The task is ours alone. I am urging only an awakening to that reality.

I am sounding a clarion call to understand and appreciate our relationship to Earth and our imperative to act accordingly. Mine is not a perspective of doom and gloom; others have followed that route and fallen short of the destination. Instead, my hope is to implore recognition and to inspire action. I want to spread the notion that every lesson for living, learning, serving, and leading is written indelibly *in* or is powerfully inspired *by* nature.

Awakening to nature does not require a trip to the Grand Canyon or a trek across the Gobi. Nature is in our back yard, a nearby city park, or a state park just down the road. Anyone can develop a relationship with nature wherever you are, a point I reiterate in each essay and a message I *exhort* in each and every nature-inspired life and living *address* I deliver. My relationship with nature is spiritual. I view my engagement as a calling, and a noble cause to sow seeds so that others might do their own part to change some small corner of this Earth for the better.

I don't claim to know the answers. I am well into the second half of my seventh decade as Earth resident. I ply my trade equipped with a forestry degree, a doctorate in applied ecology, and 45 years' experience as a practicing forester, research scientist, and university executive. I may not know the answers but I've reached a point where I can begin to articulate the questions. Learning is rooted in exploring questions. I'm living a nature-centered life. I am walking the talk of nature-inspired living and learning; all that I see, do, and say passes through a nature-lens. Daily I live the questions and seek the answers.

I write in a manner that is purpose-driven, passion-fueled, and results-oriented. The outcome I seek is that readers will live more intimately integrated with nature.

My mission is to employ writing and speaking to educate, inspire, and enable readers and listeners to understand, appreciate, and enjoy nature, and accept and practice Earth Stewardship. These are essays of passion for place and everyday nature! ...*SBJ*

"Our bondedness with the rest of creation, a sense of profound interaction, and a belief in our shared ingenuity give meaning to our lives and actions on behalf of the more-than-human world."
Lyanda Lynn Haupt

This life on Earth is a gift. We are so intricately interconnected one with another and with this land upon which we walk, build our homes, plant our gardens, and establish ourselves, that it is easy to forget how important these interrelationships are. We take for granted, for example, that each and every breath marks us as nature. Author and naturalist Lyanda Haupt reminds us of the profundity of acknowledging how integrated we are with all of "creation" and that this gives our living and behavior significance—particularly as we learn how to love and care for all that is nonhuman. For we *are* Earth. Our bones are stardust and our blood surges with the tides of salty oceans. Each one of us is unique, and utterly the same—one with the other. I mean this literally about human-to-human, but also about human-to-soil, human-to-pond, human-to-iris, human-to-robin, human-to-orca. We differentiate, group into sameness, and call out what is not "us." And in so doing we tend to forget how similar we actually are, and how sewn together we inherently exist with even those who seem utterly unfamiliar or truly unknowable: the platypus or bristlecone, the sea star or thistle, the magma or millipede.

My co-author and I have bonded for a lifetime with the various natural landscapes in which we have found ourselves. We have been taken all over the world for work, for retreat, for adventure. And in our midlife years we happened to become acquainted with one another. When we sought out a conversation, and then another and another, we found we had the basis for an abiding friendship: a rootedness in the natural world that bound us together more deeply than most. We realized that we were bound by a love for and willingness to learn from all that nature has to offer: difficulty, beauty, transitions, calm. We realized, too, that we share a love for a life of inquiry: how do we live more deeply integrated with the natural world? We decided to share our collective understandings and passions as authors of this book.

We have written this for you.

My prayer is that this book broadens you—nature lover or not—through vicarious explorations out in the natural world that you may not yet have enjoyed, but through which we (the authors) have been blessed to journey. But more than that, I hope it offers guidance and inspiration to make your own connection to Earth and all beings more tangible, more a part of daily life, richer and more dynamic. For, at the crux of every story herein, is one simple human being doing his or her utmost to deepen relationship with, learn from, and offer to the peopled world out of the bounty of the natural world. It is us sharing with you about our relationship to the creatures and landscapes, and what they have given us, so that you might be heartened to take more moments of your own life to abide with and learn from the trees, snails, mountains, waterways, and skies around you, right where you are—wherever you are. For in so doing, we believe you will find the courage to step into your own life more deeply as an Earth citizen. …*JJW*

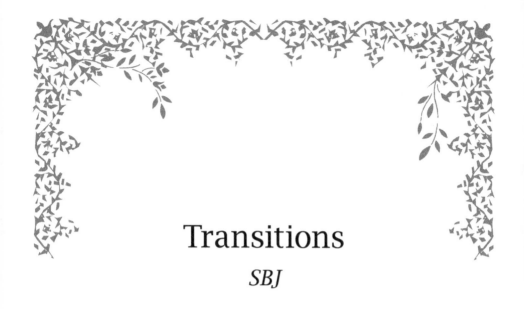

Transitions

SBJ

Transitions in nature inspire, elevate, and educate me.
Transitioning has taught me to believe, look, see, feel, and act.

I am a student of nature and, somewhat more reluctantly, of human nature. Fluxes, ebbs and flows, renewal, and senescence (natural aging and deterioration) define all living systems. They pulse and enervate seasonally, cyclically, and episodically. The same is true for physical systems: plate tectonics, deep ocean vents, hurricanes, drought, fires, solar flares, tides, and a long list of other both predictable and seemingly-random perturbations. The physical dimension intimately influences, directs, and controls biological systems. Whether we humans are leading a university, directing a global business, running a social profit organization, managing a fast food franchise, or heading a family, ebbs and flows impact all aspects of operations. Transitions, therefore, dictate decisions, or should at least modify them.

Eco-Life-System Transitions

We each traverse our years transitioning from one stage to another, some of us more than others. My maternal grandmother used to say, "The older I get, the faster time passes." I was an adolescent when her

Earth residency ended. I had no real sense of time. My life stretched ahead without end. I found her statement silly. Time is absolute, not relative, I thought. We all speed ahead at 60 minutes an hour. Time doesn't advance more quickly with age. Oh, how wrong I was back then when I knew everything!

I wrote these words at day number 113 of my 184-day tenure as six-month interim president at Fairmont State University. It can't be! Allow me a moment to reflect as time passes at near warp speed. Never have I learned so much so fast about a place, an institution, its people, its community, and its potential. My FSU tenure segmented to four stages, and perhaps five transitions. I visited June 7, 2017 as one of three finalists for interim president, just a week after setting the interview date. I quickly transitioned from Great Blue Heron CEO and author to candidate, and then to interim president-elect. Transition two began the day in mid-June when I accepted the offer and began the learning phase, which extended through mid-July. I continued learning through December 31 (my last day as interim president). By mid-July, I had transitioned to the third stage, the leading phase.

Yes, our Fairmont State University Board wisely charged me with actually *leading* that 152-year-old university, and not simply sitting in the cockpit with the plane on auto-pilot. I lettered running the mile relay in high school. I've compared my interim role to running the second or third relay leg. The first runner begins with the gun from starting blocks; the final runner crosses the finish line. The middle two accept the baton from the prior runner at top speed, and then pass it at full throttle, in the acceleration and passing (transition) zone, to the next runner.

At day 113, I was charging ahead, midway through the third and fourth turns of the quarter-mile oval. I like the relay race metaphor, yet it makes the role seem a little too simple. Even the worst track I've run was relatively smooth, reliably oval, and predictably a foot or two within 440 yards. My journey at FSU mostly fit that description, yet some stretches were more like an obstacle course, one constructed within a maze! And even a non-lethal (thankfully) landmine or two. The crowd was reasonably well behaved, and the media wonderfully kind. I slowed to clear some brush here and there, fill a pothole now and again, and help map the course ahead. I didn't set any records, nor did I stumble too badly. I relished the opportunity.

We began the fourth stage (transition) October 19, when the FSU Board of Governors announced the next president, who would accept the baton formally on January 1, 2018. We were blessed to have two months to smoothly transition. We began making plans, charting the transition course. Thankfully, the new president-elect had trained for decades. She began running her lap on January 1st. I felt eager and honored to do all that I could to ease her passage and assure that she could run her race. As we exited 2017, I transitioned back to my semi-retirement on Big Blue Lake in northern Alabama.

I have navigated many other professional transitions over 13 interstate moves, 12 years in the paper and allied products manufacturing sector, and service at nine universities. Career and professional fulfillment and advancement have guided my life's shifts. Allow me to coin a new term, borrowed from nature: eco-life-systems. I've enjoyed, studied, and managed nature's ecosystems from my undergraduate days onward. Ecosystems are somewhat fixed, and firmly rooted in place. Eco-life-systems are not. I have been nearly nomadic, moving from one eco-life-system to another.

Perhaps it is a reach to compare myself to Alaska's North Slope caribou herd. The herd spends summers protected by Arctic Ocean winds that abate the clouds of merciless bloodthirsty mosquitoes tormenting the large ungulates over tundra not ocean-proximate. When the biting insect whine diminishes, the herd ventures south to nearly the Brooks Range. The herd doesn't leave one ecosystem to venture to another; they simply wander widely across the seasons over a large area, as did the nomadic Native Alaskans who moved along with them for subsistence hunting and gathering. My moves delivered me to entirely different ecosystems, stretching from Alaska to Georgia to New Hampshire, and had nothing to do with subsistence living on the land. My subsistence came via paychecks and supermarkets. However, I suppose like the nomadic families, my impetus was Maslovian, in my case reaching beyond food and shelter to self-actualization. Regardless, I chose transition as a constant. Judy and I have lived *wide*; so many of our friends and acquaintances have lived *deep*.

Personal Transitions

Certainly, each of my eco-life-system transitions involved personal choices, yet although they did not necessarily signal a *personal* shift, they did result in such personal modification outcomes. I'll explain. I suppose I could have traipsed from position to position, and state to state as the same peculiar individual, unaffected by experience and exposure. By "personal," I refer to personality, character, intellect, demeanor, maturity, and other features that guide and illuminate our lives. For example, I entered adulthood as a certifiable introvert, fearful of public speaking, reluctant to offer serious opinions, loathe to confront, and finding comfort in close friends, deep woods, fishable waters, and forestry. I also exhibited Type A ambition (classroom, laboratory, athletic competition), rapid wit, and propensity to make people laugh. I learned after a few years of folks whom I admired mentoring and coaching me, that in addition I have a keen sense of knowing people, grasping ideas, thinking innovatively, and leading enterprises and people.

The core of who I am shifted almost imperceptibly across the years. The aggregate of who I am transitioned and matured incrementally, and mostly for the better. And now I see my leadership and communication acumen transitioning to a level and dimension orders of magnitude removed (advanced, I believe) from even a decade ago. I still employ my mind, analytic reasoning, critical thinking, and objective analyses, yet I rely upon my heart and emotion in a way that 40-year-old Steve would not have dared.

Years ago, I went to great lengths to avoid public speaking and presentations if I could. When I couldn't, I prepared detailed notes, lots of visual aids, and went mostly with objective, empirical, and scripted delivery. Today I refuse to use visual aids. I've transitioned from visual to verbal. I've discovered that such presentation aids (for me, crutches more than necessity for effective delivery) distract from the message. Every person in front of me can read, and most can read quite well. Put words on a screen, and people read them, listening marginally to what I'm saying. As for photos, I usually (but admittedly, not always) prefer to paint a verbal image. People cling to word pictures, especially when I season the presentation with heart, emotion, relevant facts, and conclusions. I avoid seasoning to excess; instead, I embrace the advice to: stand up, speak up, shut up, and sit down. I no longer fear audiences. I enjoy the challenge of understanding them and connecting with them and leaving them wishing for just a bit more. It's the same approach I adopt for leading. I've transitioned to a place where I am far more practiced and effective than ever before.

I will concede that much of what I'm describing is really personal and professional. These are learned and honed skills and abilities, strengthened through experience, gained knowledge, and the wisdom of age and application. So, I guess this type of transition is a natural, self-maturation, a form of individual life evolution. As I have written and proclaimed about such an extended learning process as is life, to maximize the absorption, consumption, and practice curve, we must be willing to employ my favorite five verbs. I've been speaking several years about *four* verbs, recently expanding to five. My overarching additional verb is *believe*. So much of what focuses my insistence upon the four verbs derives from my embrace of the power of nature-inspired life and living.

My original four verbs flow easily from that embrace. The old saw holds that *seeing is believing*; I now maintain that we can never see until we *believe*. The first of my four derived verbs is look, and awaken to our surroundings, open our eyes, clear the portals. Then, see. Engage the receptors; remove the blinders, see beneath the surface. See deeply enough to feel. Anticipate and embrace empathy and emotion for what you truly see. And lastly, feel at a depth sufficient to spur us to act. Look, see, feel, act. These four verbs alone will guide us through every transition, and even occasionally direct us to transition, if and only if we first believe. Too many people transition through the dark, blind and rudderless. Nature doesn't function that way. Intention requires a destination, a road map, and a means of transportation. Belief is the fuel that powers the transition and discovery vehicle.

Transitions in Nature

Perhaps I should have started these transition musings here. This is where my academic discipline resides. Where my heart pounds and passion surges, and what led me to my emergence as a leader, author, and speaker. Yet I wanted to get to the personal and human elements first, my own transitions.

Think for a moment of our dynamic Earth. The summit of Mount Everest is marine limestone. Calciferous sediments long ago settled to the floor of a shallow, tropical sea. Incomprehensible time and ever-deepening layers eventually buried the sea creature-remains to great depths beneath deposits heavy enough to generate enormous pressure and heat. Those conditions transformed the sediment to limestone. Then titanic crustal plate collisions (India slamming into Asia) lifted the hardened limestone nearly six miles above sea level. Today, those former tropical marine microorganisms do battle daily with bitter cold, wind, sun, snow, ice, and gravity. Nothing in nature is static; transition over time is the name of the game.

Transition over distance (both vertical and horizontal) defines ecosystems and ecosystem boundaries (ecotones). My Ph.D. research assessed the relationship between measurable site factors and forest productivity in northwestern Pennsylvania and southwestern New York. Site factors include slope steepness, slope position, slope shape, aspect, soil depth as well as mineral and chemical features, and other site attributes. Today, some 32 years hence, I see the findings as predictable and self-evident. For example, lower concave slopes (especially those facing east and north) are richer and more productive. Upper convex slopes facing south and west are the poorest. Deeper soils are more productive. Forest species composition and understory vegetation likewise shift with site.

I can't recall the nature of the forest or site where a full-grown black bear stopped by to "sample" the brown lunch-size paper bags that contained the soil horizons we had just collected from one of our plots. As we stood transfixed, the bear, finding nothing edible, ambled on, paying us little mind! But I digress. My memory of the bear is more deeply etched than that particular site or forest. A fifty-feet-away-bear encounter draws a great deal of attention. My sampling partner and I eventually *transitioned* back to the business at hand.

I do recall one particularly drastic forest transition on forestland owned by Hammermill Paper Company (my corporate host and research project funding source) above the old Austin Dam. Bayless Paper Company of Austin, PA built the concrete dam in 1890 to provide a reliable source for manufacturing process water even during periodic exceptionally dry seasons. September 1911 proved to be exceptionally wet. Flooding torrents burst the dam, destroying the mill and the town, killing 78 residents. Because concrete does not transition well to dust, the remnant dam, split and fractured, still stands at the foot of the forest transect. The concave lower slope (facing south) supported 110-foot-tall, 18-24-inch diameter red oak, black cherry, and sugar maple. Some 900-feet above, the steep convex upper slope supported only a dense thicket of 4-8-inch diameter chestnut oak. The toe-slope and ridgetop forests are the same age. The lower site is predictably far more productive.

My first book, *Nature Based Leadership*, recounts my mid-winter attempt to summit New Hampshire's Mount Washington, New England's highest peak at 6,288 feet. The lower elevations, covered in dense northern hardwood and white pine forests, held a two-foot snowpack. Scudding clouds, brisk breezes, and upper teens greeted us at the base (perhaps 1,500-foot elevation). We could see Washington's east face to 4,500-feet clearly. Above, spindrift raced across the upper slopes and summit, obscuring our view. We slowly ascended into spruce-fir forest, the trees shortening as we climbed to shrub spruce-fir, to tundra above 4,500 feet. There, the wind howled, and the blowing snow spurred donning our goggles and securing our arctic clothing. By 5,000 feet, visibility dipped in and out of zero; the ground blizzard blasted us; gusts knocked us from our feet more than once. Another two-to-three hundred feet vertical marked our apogee. We encountered fresh ten-foot drifts. The summit observatory reported winds in excess of 100 MPH and ambient temperatures well below zero. We risked life and limb by choosing other than to turn tail. Our truncated morning transect demonstrated vertical transition to the extreme, a vegetation and weather shift extraordinaire.

Not all transitions in nature extend across geography and distance. Nature's nonhuman, individual inhabitants exhibit some remarkable transitions over life spans and even seasons. We need look no further than the lepidopteran species that feed on some of my favorite eastern forest tree species: oak, cherry, and maple. From egg, to larvae, to pupae, to moth, to egg, transitions over a single lifespan yield transformations that exceed wild imagination. Imagine the horror-movie-reality of a wasp injecting her eggs (i.e. ovipositing) into a moth or butterfly larva, the eggs hatching in-situ, and the wasp larvae feeding on the host's bodily fluids from within, carefully avoiding essential organs, permitting the hapless caterpillar to itself continue feeding and growing. The wasp larvae, as their final larval act, chew through the caterpillar's tough skin, wriggle free, and immediately begin spinning cocoons. In an absolutely horrific manner (recall the *Alien* movie critter erupting from the chest cavity of host space-farers), the zombie-like caterpillar actually assists the larvae, spinning its own protective webbing around the wasp pupae. The caterpillar carcass will lie desiccated nearby when the adult wasps emerge, ready to complete the cycle by ovipositing in yet another lepidopteran larva. Ouch! I just watched a four-minute National Geographic video of the sordid process online. I am eternally grateful that my eco-life-system transitions have involved far less agony and drama!

As my stomach settles, I urge you to think, too, of longleaf pine and sand pine, two southern tree species adapted to fire ecology. Sand pine's serotinous cones, which because they are self-sealed with resin, release seed only when heat, like that generated from a wildfire, liquefies the sticky sap, permitting the cone scales to open. The seeds fall to the fire-charred, weed-consumed forest floor, find purchase, and germinate. Longleaf pine has a different fire adaptation mechanism. It drops seed annually, but its seedlings spend three to seven years in the "grass" stage, manufacturing and storing carbohydrates, anchoring a deep tap root, developing a dense root network, and growing a thick tuft of bud-protecting, grass-like needles, capable of withstanding a ground fire. When ready, the seedling bursts from the grass stage, sending its substantial growth candle vertically. In my humble view, longleaf is the most aesthetic of the southern pines. An inspiring work of nature's artwork, an amazing testament to the craft of adaptive transitions.

I've been a spring wildflower enthusiast since my sophomore spring semester when I enrolled in Dr. Glenn O. Workman's systematic botany course at Allegany Community College in western Maryland's central Appalachians. Doc introduced us early in the semester, with patches of snow lingering in the forest shade, to two rather odd flowering plants. In bogs, skunk cabbage's fleshy three-to-five-inch speckled, vessel-like flowers sat partially submerged in icy waters. Leaves nowhere in sight. The huge, cabbage-leafed foliage emerges later, when frosts and freezes are far less likely, and the reproductive pitchers begin to senesce (natural deterioration with age). The second, with its green, crook-necked stem supporting a turned-down, very-dandelion-like yellow flower, adorns the unlikeliest gravelly road shoulders, often covered and re-covered by early spring snows. The flowers close at night and refuse to open on particularly cold days. Similar in habit to the skunk cabbage, coltsfoot leaves push above ground long after the flower stems disperse their cottony seeds.

Transitions come in many forms and fashions. Salmon and other anadromous fish lead startlingly complex life cycles, beginning as fry in cold headwaters, spending much of their life in deep marine environments, and dashing at life's end to start the cycle again in the same headwaters. Certain eels lead that cycle in reverse. Terns migrate annually from high northern latitudes to similar points south and back again. Aside from breeding and fledging, life is one long, continuous transition, an eco-life-system journey.

Full Cycle Applicability

Perhaps I can say the same for my own life, although breeding played little role in selecting destinations and stop-over points. Except that we did stay at Penn State University long enough for Katy and Matt to graduate from high school: a fledging of sorts! Now, as I settle into my sunset years, my flights, migrations, and cycles see lessening amplitude and frequency. The Fairmont State University six-month interim presidency had been my first professional journey leg of predetermined duration. Really, more of an out and back side trip. I knew when I would be returning to our north-Alabama home. All other career positions came with *how long* and *what next* questions. I suppose eco-life-systems likewise have a natural transition cycle. I did not plan the amplitude and frequency on my own. I simply lived it as it developed, eagerly accepting challenge and exploiting opportunity.

I view our chosen life in the context of nature's own ebbs and flows, patterns and processes. Although the mighty oak, among my most revered of all organisms, remains steady, and anchored, I suppose that I have been more like those creatures that have evolved to adopt change as a means of livelihood and renewal. Funny that a plant guy (a forester) should choose to be nomadic, to live wide rather than deep. It's transitions in nature that inspire, elevate, and educate me. Transitioning has taught me the criticality of believing, looking, seeing, feeling, and acting. As Aldo Leopold so wisely observed in *A Sand County Almanac,* the goose who does not practice those five verbs is soon a pile of feathers. Geese know transitions far better than the wisest among us human creatures.

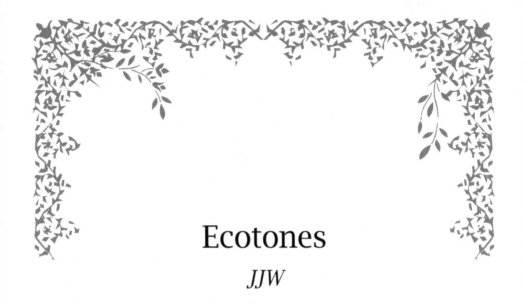

Ecotones

JJW

> An **ecotone** is a region of transition between two biological communities; a borderland, especially rich in biodiversity, containing species from each contributing biome.

Oh, how passionate I am about ecotones!

They fill me with joy, or deep abiding sorrow. No matter, they offer riches that are beyond mere emotion. I learn volumes from ecotones. I see how the concept of a borderland affirms that life is interesting, and fluid, and unsure. Like a kaleidoscope of colors and shapes, the edge between *this* and *that* is tantalizing, wavering, tangible and yet elusive, always changing. Always gorgeous. In whatever configurations the light, shadows, colors, textures create such beauty in the eyepiece of the scope, so too, ecotones tantalize.

In ecology, we use the word "ecotone" to refer to a particular region of the landscape. An ecotone is a transition zone, a place where two or more distinct biological communities come together (like the area where a forest transitions to a meadow). An ecotone is especially rich in biodiversity because it contains species from each natural area that converges there. The ecotone between the forest and meadow might contain small grasses, a few scattered saplings, wildflowers and some blown leaf litter, for example. They are juicy areas of confluence. An ecotone is not one natural area or the other; it is bits of both. We can also think about ecotones as: edges, boundaries, regions of confluence, borders, transition zones, areas of overlap. Sometimes it is difficult to determine where one biome ends and the next begins; but it is very easy to see, *farther out on the landscape*, where each is its own distinct entity. These margins can be very gradual, incredibly subtle; they are not the black line marking a boundary on a map. Ecotones exist where natural communities have merged over space (and time, of course); the term, then, is largely a spatial referent. It is the union, the seam, between one and the other.

When I first heard the term "ecotone" at the beginning of my graduate studies, I inexplicably felt like I had come home. The concept of 'extraordinary richness in a transition place' resonated deeply within me. I love word games and conceptual challenges, making sense of my experience of life through metaphor, simile, and abstract ideas. Somehow even back then when midlife had not yet descended upon me in irreversible cycles of physical, relational, and ideological changes, I knew that using the term 'ecotones' as a representative for the special diversity and significance of particular aspects of life *as a human* held great potential.

It is no wonder that my graduate studies merged several disciplines into one; the rich terrain between human culture and the natural environment was the focal point for each major research project I undertook. My Master's level work looked at the ecotone of inner transformation that conjoins with intercultural ecotours; my doctoral work more deeply examined these issues by specifying the interface of crafts cooperatives and environmental conservation as the ecotone under study. Interdisciplinary approaches to problems in academia, fields of study that merge two previously distinct methodologies, even research paradigms that see the researcher as both observer and participant can be rich places that contain much more than single-pointed approaches can hold.

Actually, my little home is just yards away from an ecotone. From my desk I can look out the window and see three isolated banana-yellow skunk cabbage blossoms coming up through last year's dried grasses and underbrush between the mowed grass and the mixed alder-conifer forest patch. Some creatures pay no attention to their "rightful" habitat-ecozone. A pair of mallards has come strutting through the mowed grass following a soggy stream that inadvertently and yet with determination pays no attention to boundaries either; the ducks and the water-flowing-as-mud through the lawn don't seem to care that the stream proper flows eight feet to the west. Neither do the several skunk cabbage plants worry that the clump of perfectly sodden habitat where dozens of their relatives are thriving is just over yonder.

Imagine with me for a moment a landscape devoid of ecotones, one in which boundaries (like a god-sized permanent Magic Marker) are indelibly marked with fat painted lines. What we would have, instead, at the edge of the forest before the designated meadow begins might be bare ground, continually weeded to keep out plant growth. So, we would have the forest. Then a strip of soil that is a fixed width (say, perhaps, twelve inches). On the other side of the dividing line would be the meadow filled with tall grasses of many varieties, flowers and insects along with the rest of the grassland inhabitants: ants and bees, snakes, voles, rabbits, and hawks circling from above, perhaps. But where the artificial boundary gets drawn is impossible to determine. For example, insects (crawling as well as flying ones) pay no heed to boundary lines, nor do they avoid flying across into the forest. A hawk flies low over the swaying tops of the grasses and crosses over boundaries between meadow and forest in pursuit of the scampering mouse that is dashing across the bare Earth toward the forest. We can't make such artificial boundaries. It is a blessing as well as a shortcoming that we humans make such determinations. But thank goodness for ecotones, those naturally existing transitions that allow for fluidity and thriving life.

As an Idea

Conceptually, the term "ecotone" offers a more complex perspective of how things *really* manifest in life. If we think about the term "ecotones" as an idea that is defined by those characteristics of a transition zone in the natural world, we can begin to apply this understanding to our lives. Ecotones, then, can be instructive for areas of our lives that move beyond natural communities and spatial zones; ecotones can help us understand the emotional and spiritual transitions on our inner landscapes as well. There is hope and inspiration in the idea of ecotones as applied to the transitions of the human life. The qualities of an ecotone are: two or more things coming together; lack of a fixed, rigid line separating the two entities; a gradual transition between one and the other; and increased diversity due to the presence of characteristics from both. Ecotones *as a concept* could refer to the union of at least two things gradually coming together over space and time, and during which the presence and qualities of past and future commingle in the present in a potentially enriching manner. In short, ecotones can be used conceptually to refer to transitions of all sorts.

A simple comparison, and one with which we are all familiar, is the change of seasons. In the natural world the temperatures slowly begin to rise or fall, precipitation gradually changes, the grasses and leaves are altered, and there are shifts in terms of which particular bird species are present. We might not want to overlook, either, the ways in which *we* shift with the seasons; our animal selves with natural instincts unfettered also turn inward in winter, begin to emerge freshly in spring, are out and about in summer, and begin to move closer to home in autumn.

The boundary between one and the other is not absolutely demarcated.

What I find compelling about ecotones as a concept is that they offer us a new way to live; they teach us how rich life transitions are; they afford us some leeway so that everything *doesn't* have to fit into tidy boxes of definition and structure. Ecotones model the richness of confluence and therefore inspire us to embrace the complexities that life hands to us each day. Events, difficulties, and relationships lose their need to be labeled as *this* or *that*; the structures of easy definitions fall away and we learn to sit with what is. Even inquiry is freer when we use ecotones as a metaphor for living: no longer do answers provide the sole consolation; ecotones show us that the richness lies in the complexity of not knowing, in the act of inquiry itself. It points us toward a more fluid, dynamic interstice where each moment offers just that which is required to proceed forward. If we can open fully to the questions and dilemmas we face, I heartily believe that each moment will offer the wisdom we need to proceed with compassion. Of course, this requires that we allow the soul's insight to share air-time with our intellect. We need both the landscape of the mind and the terrain of the heart to guide us in these complex times; we need to embrace that place where intellect and compassion converge. Just like ecotones.

Some Examples

I can draw an example of this from the two decades I've worked as a hospice volunteer. Hospice work has a powerful allure for me; we work at the known ecotone between "life" and "death." It is the transition time between what we understand as *living* (here on Earth) and *dying*: that final and seemingly-permanent ending. There is both *living* and *dying* happening during the designated time between prognosis (irreversible illness that will be fatal in approximately six months) and death. For example, many of the people who are dying with whom I have worked might be especially energized around life review: going over those aspects of one's life that were especially meaningful or significant. This poignant and hugely significant end-of-life work includes tasks such as: remembering how one's life was unique; making amends with the important people in their life; spending as much time with loved ones as possible; saying goodbye; and leaving a legacy of life in the form of story, photos, or other compiled mementos. While all this energizing activity is going on (living each moment as fully and present as possible), there is still the body declining, dying. Slow changes are occurring such as reduced capability to perform simple self-care tasks, loss of the use of particular limbs or body parts, reduced cognitive functioning, decreased stamina. This dying person, then, is living (eating, breathing, engaging with self and others) and dying (physically shutting down), *simultaneously.*

This is the rich ecotone between life and death. At hospice, we are given the great blessing of knowing we are in this transition zone, the boundary between living now and death soon. (One doesn't have to be on hospice service to have an ecotone, a boundary place, between life and death; we all have this, but in hospice it is known and relatively fixed in a temporal sense.)

Creativity is another example of how ecotones can be understood as a concept. Collages are a visual portrayal of the ecotonal characteristic of "two or more aspects of each coming together into one." I have been dabbling in collage-making for nearly twenty years. The collage pieces I make are usually a combination of handcrafted paper, adhesive, natural materials (leaves, bark, twigs, flowers, grass, moss, fur, bones) and the substrate on which the collage materials are adhered. The disparate materials come together into a single whole. The most aesthetically-pleasing areas of the collage are those where several different materials overlap, offering something new as they conjoin. Ecotones are those places where one community transitions to another. Collages manifest this inherently in two ways: there are the various materials coming into relationship with one another (green paper, seed husks, ribbon, a dried pansy), and there is the actual process of creativity (which is the ecotone, or transition, between creative inspiration and the created object).

Often, the transitions in our lives do not exist in a vacuum. We experience changes over time, and sometimes over space; we can understand these as "ecotones" too. We can begin to view those areas of our lives that are difficult, challenging, or not easily definable, as crucial areas of our lives. I know that transitions in my life can be an especially anxiety-laden time. Whether it is a transition between jobs, homes, or life stages; spiritual changes as one's faith or religious practices shift; or emotional changes such as those accompanying the major milestones in life (e.g., birth, graduation, retirement), there is often no immediate change but rather a steady progression from one aspect of life to the next. And, we need for the transitions in our lives *to be gradual* in order for us to have time to acclimate, to adjust, to the terrain.

As humans, we are not very good at living with the unknown or precarious in life. When I have overheard or participated in conversations in which somebody is detailing the life transition in which she finds herself, it often ends with clean platitudes by the listener. They go something like this: *Don't worry. You'll be through this in no time.* In other words, "Pretty soon everything in your life will be fixed, static, and predictable again." (Until it's not, which is inevitable.) We are creatures in flux; the very notion of life implies transition, change, evolution, degradation, movement, activity, transformation. "Stasis," "fixed," or "sameness" do not figure in to that list.

As a meditator, I find that presence in this moment *right now* is one way to wrap my arms around life as it unfolds; this is yet another example of how life mimics the characteristics of ecotones. Sitting quietly, still, and watching my breath—inhalation, exhalation—brings me to this moment in time and space. Rather than focusing on what was (the past) or what is coming (tomorrow, ten years from now), I am beginning to understand just how profound and full this hour is. My eyes glance up from my computer screen as the movements outside alert me to the virile birdlife and beauty of this sunshiny spring day. My breath catches as I behold the simple robin, four worms in her mouth; I ponder where her nest might be, how many little chicks she is feeding with those fat wriggling worms. I hear the robins' raucous calls and remember that their wingbeats flying just above my head yesterday made a small roaring *swhoosh!* In the instant that I move into memory, I have lost this moment now. A Buddhist teacher with whom I often sat in meditation said that remembering isn't the actual experience itself. *Remembering* the robins' flight overhead is not the actuality of having the wingbeats hovering inches above; instead "remembering" is that set of *thoughts about* that experience. When I remember to be present right now, with what is unfolding before my window, my computer screen, the feel of my breath as it moves in and out, then I am living fully and with presence. Every moment can be an ecotone, a transition, from this to the next. Every bit of our lives can be that rich, diverse transition zone from past to future. If we live in the present moment, we are living in the ecotone of our lives. I am not shying away from the crimp in my neck from sitting too long at the computer, the exhaustion from moving boxes and furniture into my new home, the myriad details associated with a job change, or even the seasonal fluctuations during which I carry a variety of outer wraps to accommodate weather variations in any given day.

These remind me that ecotones—by definition, rich transition zones—exist in daily life.

Living into Ecotones

Ecotones continue to enthrall me!

Until twenty years ago, I never had a word for the area that exists between a forest and a meadowland, or the sand dunes and the high tide line. In fact, because I didn't have a word to describe and define the zone between the two, I became blind to those areas. It was as if the sea and the dune were either one and the same (which seemed impossible to me) or completely different and unconnected. But transitional zones imply just that: a process of getting from one thing to the next. They connect. I kept looking for the actual place where I could stand and say "Okay, I'm at the beach," or, "Now I'm standing on the dune." The bliss in finding out that the physical location of "beach" and "dune" is less easily demarcated put me at ease. Rather than confusing me, the lack of definitive, pinpointed "end" and "beginning" corroborated my inner experience of how life *really* flows; I have come to increasingly take great comfort in this.

The ideas about and characteristics of ecotones are not perfectly or literally equated with transitions or diversity. Rather, they teach us to stretch our habitual orientation to life and change so that we begin to see transitions as rich, useful, necessary, inevitable, and beautiful. They remind us to appreciate those aspects of living that tend to cause us discomfort, that are often riddled with tension because they put us on the edge of something, rather than locating us squarely in the center of whatever we consider our "life." Except that transitions *are* our life; we are always in flux and movement. To be static is to be dead.

How can we use these notions, drawing from the examples above, to live our lives in a snug embrace of the reality of our existence? How can we move from concept to action? In what ways can we begin to shift our perspective so that those things which we find challenging— because they are not still or fixed—become a celebratory cherishing of this moment right now?

Living in the ecotone of our lives means showing up fully to every blessing and challenge that is offered to us in these years, months, days, hours and the specks of moments between this activity and the next one. Embracing the ecotones, those minute and vast temporal spaces that are not clearly *this* or *that*, is how we really experience the richness of life. It is the interstices of our lives that matter as much as the end points. It is not the journey, rather than the destination we are to embrace (as the cliché says); the journey *is* the end point: it is all we have. Right now. The journey is happening with every breath we take (or each one we hold); the long exhale of a stressful sigh is as much to behold as the one which holds clarity and resolution of "the problem." Embodying the abundance and diversity, the ongoing changes, the place in between the distinct aspects of our lives is how we live in the ecotones.

So, like that nebulous space between the sand dune and the high tide line, our lives are made up of indistinct borders and boundaries; the lines are not fixed between one stage and the next (…marriage and divorce, conception and birth, prognosis and death, puberty, emergent ideas, spiritual growth…). We can see clearly behind us and with hopes ahead of us, but it is only right now that we can feel with any assuredness. It is only this ecotone place with all its riches that we can claim. The spatial reality of an ecological ecotone informs us as we move through the temporal ecotones of our lives.

Living in the ecotone of our lives means acknowledging that the overlapping area between not knowing (discomfort) and knowing (ease) is profuse with both the shadows (those things we find unpleasant but don't really deal with) and the light. We can practice allowing the naturally-occurring richness of the unknown—that place where darkness and brightness can exist in harmony—to be there in full acknowledgment. We can take guidance from the "meeting ground" between what is known and that which is not yet known. The ecotone is the fertile ground of self-examination, taking stock of what we can do to move toward more of an embrace of what *is*, living fully with all the uncertainties and dilemmas but also finding balance between stasis and action.

As a personal example, I beseech myself daily to find the rich terrain that inhabits and connects somewhere between throwing up my hands saying, "It's too late; we're going to hell in a handbasket!" and the need to be an environmental savior.

We "practice" being in the place of not having all the answers by remembering to see the "juicy richness" inherently there as fodder for right action. We simply sit with the pain, the realities, the challenges, the potential for wholeness without the incessant action of text messaging, cell phones, emails, blogs and websites and googling, theaters and televisions, and total technological connectedness. A re-embrace of the non-electronic world can remind us of who we are and thus remind us of our rightful place on this planet. This is not to polarize against technology but to remember how to use it *in harmony with* time on the land. I cannot feel a sense of my interconnectedness with all beings, or my rightful place on the planet, by staying here at this computer, with the cell phone ringing. I need to walk the land finding that incredibly fertile ground between myself and the nonhumans, between work and ease.

Living in the ecotone of our lives means pondering a deeper understanding of what actions are needed as we take our place as responsible global environmental residents. Seeing the dead great blue heron washed up on the beach near my house yesterday; watching the geoduck diggers at low tide; watching the crow steal the robin chick from the nest earlier this morning; observing how long it takes for the buds to unfurl into the vibrant, green leaves of this springtime, or which windows the full moon brightens during different seasons of the year; noticing the various ways in which the river otter, varied thrush, pair of mallard ducks, coyote, raccoon family, and great bald eagle move through the grass in the yard outside my window. I smell the changes in seasons as I hike the trail adjacent to my home. I can feel the cold breeze on my skin indicating—more accurately than the thermometer— which jacket I'll need to don today. These small things I engage with each day give me a chance to practice finding my rightful place, being in the moment, embracing all that I don't know, feeling the pains and glory of this life on Earth.

Living in the ecotone of our lives means opening our hearts to ourselves and to all beings, placing us squarely on the path that will lead us toward balanced harmony and constructive action. It also means relinquishing extremes of belief (pitting one thing against another). I love this E.B. White quote: "I wake up each morning torn between a desire to save the world and a desire to savor the world. This makes it very hard to plan the day." What lies between saving and savoring is compassion.

The only truly viable option I see is to lead with our hearts; to admit our human frailties, fears, and ignorance; to acknowledge the divine and the wise inherent in nature. May our presence, acknowledgment, and pondering—combined with a hearty dose of compassion—lead us through the ecotones of our lives in order that we realize our effective action on behalf of this planet of beautiful beings.

In our embrace of ecotones, may we find the courage to live fully. In these, I find inspiration and hope.

Nature's Islands

SBJ

"Look again at that dot. That's here. That's home. That's us.
On it everyone you love, everyone you know, everyone you ever
heard of, every human being who ever was, lived out their lives.
The aggregate of our joy and suffering, thousands of confident
religions, ideologies, and economic doctrines, every hunter and
forager, every hero and coward, every creator and destroyer of
civilization, every king and peasant, every young couple in love,
every mother and father, hopeful child, inventor and explorer,
every teacher of morals, every corrupt politician, every 'superstar,'
every 'supreme leader,' every saint and sinner in the history of our
species lived there - on a mote of dust suspended in a sunbeam."
Carl Sagan

I want more people to comprehend the threat and the promise facing our
species on island-Earth. To feel deeply enough to evoke action ... action
to fuel the fierce green fire of human sustainability on a planet rich with
the integrity, stability, and beauty of Earth's island-wide biotic community!

Dictionary.com defines *island* as: "a tract of land completely
surrounded by water, and not large enough to be called a continent;
something resembling an island, especially in being isolated or having
little or no direct communication with others."

Islands come in all manners, shapes and sizes. At the extreme, our Earth is an island, isolated in space and by time, and having no direct communication with others. We Americans launched the Voyager space probe 41 years ago. It has just now reached beyond our solar system, logging some 14 billion miles. Sounds like a considerable distance. Were we to direct an Earth-origin beam of light at the center of our Milky Way Galaxy, its photons would reach that destination in 25,000 years (traveling at 186,000 miles per second). On the same trajectory and at its current pace, Voyager would complete its journey in 434 million years! Earth is an island.

Yet occasionally we read of an asteroid striking Earth: an intracosmic traveler penetrating our atmosphere with pieces of it making it to Earth's surface. The age of dinosaurs apparently ended when a greater object (mountain-size) collided with us. It is possible that a long time ago in a galaxy far, far away, a similar collision occurred, shattering a verdant Earth-like planet and jettisoning large fragments into deep space. Perhaps one such piece collided with our then life-free, iron-core Earth four billion or so years ago, bearing a few life-fragments frozen and suspended in time. Perhaps our barren island in the sky accepted life from another source, serving as an incubator for that alien life to resurrect and evolve. Or perhaps another intelligent life form saw promise in the raw planet Earth and sowed seed. Whether of secular or religious origins, life today flourishes on Earth, our own mote of dust.

My point is not so much to speculate on the origin of life on Earth as to ponder whether there is such a construct as a true island, totally and absolutely isolated across time and the universe. For the purposes of this chapter, let's assume that Earth was, is, and always shall be an island. Within that assumption, I re-enter today's Earth and the life we know. Islands, island ecology, and partitions do, in fact, influence and bear meaning for us.

Islands Real and Perceived

"There are degrees and kinds of solitude. An island in a lake has one kind; but lakes have boats, and there is always the chance that one might land to pay you a visit. A peak in the clouds has another kind; but most peaks have trails, and trails have tourists. I know of no solitude so secure as one guarded by a spring flood; nor do the geese, who have seen more kinds and degrees of aloneness than I have.

So we sit on our hill beside a new-blown pasque, and watch the geese go by. I see our road dipping gently into the waters, and I conclude (with inner glee but exterior detachment) that the question of traffic, in or out, is for this day at least, debatable only among carp."

Aldo Leopold, *A Sand County Almanac*

Leopold knew of islands literal and symbolic, temporal and static, physical and emotional. He wrote prose poetically and brought magic to isolation, even as he celebrated aloneness as a seasonal elixir that he shared with spring's geese and the foraging carp. If only my pen issued such magic!

I won't presume to present all manner of islands to you. Allow me instead to wander (and wonder) to just a few. Although I present these as distinct and separate categories, please know that each one shares common core with the others.

Climatic Islands

The most recent North American continental ice sheet began its retreat some 15-20,000 years ago, its mid-continent lobe having extended from St. Louis east-north-eastward to Long Island, itself a significant terminal moraine. I conducted my doctoral research on the Allegheny Plateau in northwestern Pennsylvania and southwestern New York, highlands that held the glacial front at bay, diverting it west and east, much as water to a boulder in a stream. There were no glacial till and outwash derived soils in my study area. However, the several-thousand-feet-high glacial front stood just to the north, creating a periglacial climate that left evidence in boulder flows, soils marked by solifluction, deep freezing, and tundra vegetation.

The persistent cold that enabled the glacial genesis and advance reached deeply into lower latitudes. Boreal forests and taiga surged southward as climate changed and the ice advanced. Canadian forests found themselves flourishing in the southern Appalachians. When warmth slowly returned, the northern vegetation marched back toward its higher latitudes. These are not human snowbird paced migrations. These changes occurred over millennia, in fact they continue today. The retreat left islands of boreal forests and taiga at higher elevations from the Great Smoky Mountains north.

Mount Mitchell in North Carolina provides a Canadian species treasure trove for the southern botanist unable to transit 1,000+ miles to the north. Simple atmospheric physics enable those relict ecosystems to persist at elevation. Average annual temperature decreases with elevation. Spring advances (and fall progresses in reverse) vertically at about one week per 800 feet. The similar rule of thumb for latitude is one week per hundred miles. Mount Mitchell's latitudinal equivalent takes us a couple of hundred miles into Ontario! The actual equivalent is compounded by the harsh winds and storms at 6,684 feet atop Mitchell. It's a rough world on the highest *island* east of the Mississippi!

I'll borrow an island-in-the-sky example from an essay in my second book, *Nature-Inspired Learning and Leading*, to further emphasize the local consequences and implications of elevation:

> *Mount Marshall at 3,368 feet stands sentinel along the northern Blue Ridge, prominent from our Wisdom Center sun porch view to the WSW across the fields. Our perch atop Viewtree Mountain (1,050 feet) sits 500 feet above and a couple of miles west of Warrenton, Virginia, accessed via Hesperides Road's multiple switchbacks climbing from Bear Wallow Road. Twelve line-of-sight miles from us, Marshall's nearly one-half-mile vertical advantage draws our view. While spring's green graces Viewtree's hilltop yellow poplars, we can see that verdant tints reach only Marshall's lower slopes.*

Because spring travels vertically at a rate of one week per 800-feet vertical, Mount Marshall stood roughly three weeks behind us in spring's advance. Imagine a map of seasonal contour lines, depicting Marshall as an island of late winter above a sea of spring.

Mountains everywhere wring moisture from air passing over them and create rain shadows in their lee. Near my central-Appalachian home, the Allegany Front (2,800-3,600 feet elevation) annually tallies 50+ inches of precipitation. The lower ridge and valley province just to the east records 10-15 inches less. The Cascades draw tremendous moisture from the prevailing wet-westerlies from the Pacific. High desert country lies not far to the east. Puerto Rica's east-end, montane rainforests lie within just a few miles of the dry lee side. Climatic islands are common. Flora, fauna, and life at all scales vary from place to place.

An *urban heat island* is another category of climatic island. Native vegetation here in the eastern U.S. transpires (the plant process of transferring moisture from the soil through the plant to the atmosphere) tremendous quantities of water, each molecule that evaporates doing its small part to cool the atmosphere. Conversion of forest to buildings and pavement eliminates that powerful cooling effect. Dark pavement and rooftops absorb and store solar insolation otherwise reflected by vegetation; try walking across a parking lot barefooted. Internal combustion engines generate heat; try touching a car's manifold. Waste energy dissipates from power lines. Heat leaks from homes and businesses. Urban areas can experience temperatures elevated by 3-7 degrees Fahrenheit from their rural surroundings.

Literal Islands

Darwin's adventures courtesy of the HMS Beagle shed light on the island effect. Isolate a population over time and change and adaptation express differentially. His findings apply to isolation whether it be islands separated by water or other factors. Jared Diamond wrote of the ultimate collapse of Easter Island's advanced civilization owing to island isolation and non-sustainable agronomic practices.

Easter Island's doomed civilization faced the same predicament Sagan applied to our planetary situation: "In our obscurity - in all this vastness - there is no hint that help will come from elsewhere to save us from ourselves. It is up to us." Only vestiges of that civilization remain; help did not come from elsewhere.

Ecological Islands

The extinct Ivory-billed woodpecker depended upon large tracts of mature bottomland hardwood forests in the southern U.S. "The realm of the ivory-bill consisted primarily of the swamps and river bottom woods within the vast forest that stretched across the deep South west to eastern Texas and north to Missouri, southern Illinois, southern Indiana and southern Ohio." (*Hope is the Thing with Feathers*, Christopher Cokinos). Cokinos quoted Jacob Studer's 1881 *Studer's Popular Ornithology: The Birds of North America*, describing those forests as "gloomy swamps and morasses overshadowed by dark, gigantic cypresses, stretching their bare and blasted branches, as it were, midway to the skies." Drainage for conversion to agriculture reduced the acreage below the species' threshold. Sketches, grainy photographs, paintings, and a few old taxidermy mounts remind us painfully of what we have lost. From the vast ocean of favorable habitat only islands remain. Insufficient to sustain this once common grand denizen, this "Lord-God" bird, this second largest woodpecker on the planet, the broken and fragmented forest eventually resonated one final time with the bird's futile plea.

The gopher tortoise, a threatened reptile, occupies special site niches from southeastern Louisiana through Mississippi, Alabama, Georgia, and Florida, sandy uplands suitable for the tortoise's burrowing lifestyle. When I served as Union Camp Corporation's Alabama Region Land Manager, we identified and protected colonies, treating them with respect and care. In effect, theirs is an island habitat, isolated by large acreages of non-suitable habitat.

We likewise identified and protected colonies of the endangered red cockaded woodpecker, observing on our own land those guidelines established by the U.S. Fish and Wildlife Service. The birds depend upon mature forests of principally longleaf pine. If only we had acted in time to save the ivory-bill! The world is rich with species whose habitat is under siege, to include neotropical songbirds, monarch butterflies, and countless others. We still have a chance to do it right for those species in peril, but I cannot speculate on how much longer we have to act. Earth is an island with geographic fractals across its surface. We do not yet adequately understand island biogeography to ensure species survival. And even if and when we do, I'm not sure that we as a society will act to protect life on Earth (and humanity) from ourselves.

Continental Isolation

Our pale blue orb owes its moniker to the three-quarters of Earth's surface covered by oceans. Since Pangaea began drifting apart to create today's continents, the oceans have effectively isolated macroscopic lifeforms of Europe, Asia, and Africa from the Americas and from Australia. Airborne microorganisms likely transited the oceans. But the megafauna and floral forms evolved separately over the sweep of time since the super-continent parted. Even *Homo sapiens* did not make the Americas until crossing the Bering land bridge during the most recent ice age, and there remaining isolated since the ice's retreat until seafaring nations crossed the open waters during this present millennium (Vikings, English, Italians, Spaniards).

Woe be to the long-established populations stemming from the Bering bridge crossing. Europeans brought organisms to which Native Americans were not adapted, measles, influenza, typhus fever, and smallpox among them. Some sources report that introduced pathogens killed two of every three Native Americans.

Europeans brought more than human pathogens. The list of pests and pestilence agent freeloaders is long. Consider a few: stink bugs, Japanese beetles, killer bees, gypsy moths, emerald ash borer, chestnut blight, Dutch elm disease, smutty nose of bats, zebra mussels, rats, starlings, purple loosestrife, dandelion, bush honeysuckle, phragmites, Bradford pear, kudzu, anaconda in the Everglades, and countless more.

Reflections

Planes, trains, trucks, and boats have shrunk our home planet. Nothing is totally isolated. Only a single island remains, Earth itself. Now more than ever, John Muir's words hold true: "When we try to pick out anything by itself, we find it hitched to everything else in the Universe."

Ours is a global biome. We 7.7 billion human inhabitants share one atmosphere, a single interconnected ocean system, a common hydrologic cycle, and a future globally interdependent with the past and present. We are both protagonist and antagonist, both victim and assailant. We have only this one chance to get it right. It matters not if only some of us act responsibly. The collective bears the burden.

John Donne immortalized a given:

"No man is an island,

Entire of itself,

Every man is a piece of the continent,

A part of the main"

Likewise, no nation, continent, or community is an island. Whether viewed by astrophysicist or poet, we humans are in this together. We are one with the Earth. We cannot escape the reality. We no longer have the luxury of actual escape from life's brutal harshness that Simon and Garfunkel proclaimed in *I Am a Rock*:

"A winter's day

In a deep and dark December;

I am alone,

Gazing from my window to the streets below

On a freshly fallen silent shroud of snow.

I am a rock,

I am an island."

They concluded, "a rock feels no pain, an island never cries." Societally, we risk both pain and tears if we fail to heed the warning signals from an Earth called upon to provide ever-greater goods and services. Earth itself is not endangered. She and life (in some form or fashion) on it will persist until our sun dims or, in the process of dimming, expands to vaporize our pale blue orb. Or until another mountain-size galactic fragment collides with us. Far short of such certain planetary demise, we humans can foul our earthly nest to the point it cannot sustain us. Earth will scarcely note, nor long remember, our species' brief flourish.

We may make a faint impression in the future fossil library. Sediments from our reign may evidence the record of our products of combustion. Strange alloys and compounds may bear witness to our innovations and creations. And plastic residue may appear ubiquitous during the flash-in-time of our appearance. As I wrote this passage, Hawaii's Big Island Kilauea volcano was grunting, groaning, spewing, and adding new mass. The relatively mild lava production was a big deal for those living nearby. However, over the sweep of time, the activity is nothing. The ocean crust sliding over the geologic hot spot will in time shift island-building to the east-southeast. Even the Big Island will weather into the Pacific. Islands, like our lives, are temporal as well as physical.

John McPhee noted in *Basin and Range*, "If by some fiat I had to restrict all this writing to one sentence, this is the one I would choose: The summit of Mt. Everest is marine limestone." That single statement symbolizes the endless cycles of life and living, sustaining across the eons. Everest's peak comprises calcareous rock seeded long ago in a warm, shallow sea of debris, in part washed from ancient mountains long since eroded by agents of relentless destruction. Today's fresh Kilauea lava will waste into the sea and may someday rise as sedimentary rock to 29,000-feet above sea level.

Learning from Nature

We must understand and accept our place on this precious planet and recognize our utter dependence upon it. We may be the only species ever to occupy Earth with the capacity to self-destruct. I don't mean just militarily. Sagan nailed it: as far as we know, rescue from elsewhere is not at hand. I am not leaping to a gloom and doom scenario outcome. Mercifully, we are also likely Earth's first inhabitants with intelligence sufficient to comprehend our self-imposed risks and dilemma, and to take action to intercede on behalf of future generations. The first step toward addressing any problem is realization. My immediate objective is to assist us in moving beyond denial.

I am not talking about specific causes, human-induced climate change, for example. I am not a climate scientist. I leave the science, politics, agenda, and emotions to others. I do know that the concept of carrying capacity is real, and deeply at play for humans on Earth. And the application goes well beyond simply sustaining human life at some level. For me, life without quality is a diminished existence. I have no desire to reside on an island devoid of fresh air, aesthetic reward, clean water, and all manner of wildness. Aldo Leopold expressed my own sentiment: "There are some who can live without wild things and some who cannot." Like Leopold, I am one who cannot.

I wish to draw two conclusions. First, islands are real as well as metaphorical, absolute and subjective, mostly static in human-life terms yet temporal over Earth-time, small-scale and in fractals extending to planet-dimension. We humans must think ultimately of our Earth-island. Nothing smaller matters in the long run. Once again, Leopold offered deep ecological and philosophical wisdom via *A Sand County Almanac and Sketches Here and There*, my secular Bible:

> "A thing is right when it tends to preserve the integrity, stability and beauty of the biotic community. It is wrong when it tends otherwise."

Any island, be it the domain atop Viewtree Mountain or our planet Earth, has worth and value to us only if we preserve and protect the integrity, stability, and beauty of the biotic community. I fear that humanity is at risk, in isolation from nature, and in ignorance or denial of our absolute dependence upon Earth.

Leopold wrote in *A Sand County Almanac* of shooting a wolf and making it to the animal as it expired, and seeing the fierce green fire of her eyes fade in death. He wrote of the episode many years later, lamenting the action of his "trigger-itch" days, when he viewed wolves as anathema to healthy and vibrant deer herds. I wonder how many among us, 70 years beyond Leopold's death, sense that it is we humans whose *fierce green fire* may be in peril.

One of my primary goals for writing and speaking is to rekindle and stoke the fire of recognition and concern that burned within Leopold, passing the torch to American and global citizens and leaders. To assure that wolf, mountain, and man recognize and sustain the power and wisdom in those long-ago wolf eyes. Again, islands are real and metaphysical, illuminated by the essential fierce green fire. For it is only through keeping the flame real and paramount that we can sustain meaningful life for future human generations on planet Earth, our one island that matters.

My second primary conclusion is that Earth is an island ecosystem. All parts and elements are interconnected and interdependent. I admit to harboring a lifelong disgust of cigarettes. A former marathon runner, I deplore their vile odor and the symbol of pulmonary and related diseases they incite. My dad smoked and suffered breathing complications that shortened his life. I mention my disgust as a vehicle for making a relevant point. I recall the days when airplanes had smoking sections, as though the smoke-congested air stayed in place and the rest of us did not have to inhale the particulates and carcinogens. It's like declaring a no-peeing end of the community pool!

Our Earth is like the plane and pool, an integrated system. We are a plastic-dependent society. We employ its magic and convenience on land even as it clogs our oceans. We generate industrial and automobile exhaust from mid-latitudes; particulates reduce Arctic ice-field albedo (measure of surface reflectivity). Ours is a planetary mixing bowl, a global ecosystem. We must be ever-aware that all is one, and all must act as one and for one. One Earth.

I hope that we can we push through our denial, accept responsibility, and pursue action. We occupy a planetary Easter Island. Once it is too late, we will leave little more than mysterious statuary on a pale blue island in the vast darkness of space. Such remarks seem dire, fatalistic, and without hope. Yet, we do have the capacity to sustain, provided we generate the will. I know few people who are aware that we humans could be the global ivory-bill, the extinct Lord-God bird.

I often ponder what more I can do to help us Think Like a Mountain, how I might ignite awareness of the fierce green fire. I want more people to believe that our Earth-island's ecological salvation is within reach. And to realize that Nature's wisdom and power, through a deliberate ecosystem approach, can ensure our future. I want more people to look inquiringly for the depth of our dilemma. To occasionally put aside their digital distractions. And to look deeply enough to see both our dilemma and our hope. I want more people to comprehend the threat and the promise. To feel deeply enough to evoke action, action to fuel the fierce green fire of human sustainability on a planet rich with the integrity, stability, and beauty of Earth's island-wide biotic community!

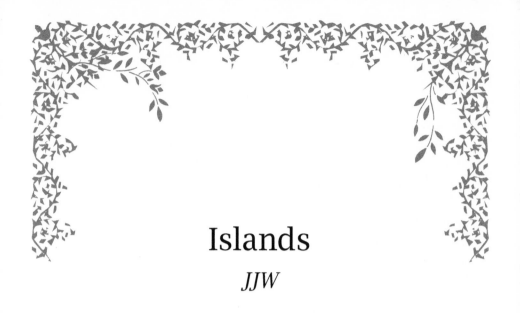

Islands

JJW

Islands are tracts of land that are smaller than a continent and which are surrounded by water.

I've been intrigued with the "idea" of islands for most of my life. Michener's *Hawaii* seemed a bit too daunting that summer after my first year of college, when I thought I'd read all the great writers in my early desire to be an author; the sheer volume of it weighed down my daypack on hikes through the Rocky Mountains. A year or two after college, when I had moved to the Pacific Northwest and was living on the edge of downtown Seattle, I got to hear Oliver Sacks speak for the first time and I was enamored; his blend of science-made-accessible and compelling stories about patients with every manner of neurological problem deeply captured my attention. (At the time, I was working with youth with special needs, many of whom had neurological disorders of various types.) I decided to read Sacks' work and immediately purchased a copy of *The Island of the Colorblind*. I was rapt with the first part of the book which featured a remote island in the Pacific on which most of the islanders were born with total colorblindness. I also admit to being drawn in my youth to songs like Garfunkel's *I Am a Rock*. I fancied I was a hermit in the making (understanding nothing at the time about my introversion), and with my sense of fierce independence would be able to survive any calamity—physical or emotional—merely on my wits and tenacity; I've learned a lot since then, primarily: that we need one another, we need community, we need shared sorrows and shared joys. Though I still now and again revisit the romantic aspects of my hermit idea, I have come to believe in the power of interconnection. During my graduate school years, I was spellbound by David Quammen's *The Song of the Dodo*. A tome in and of itself (but still only three-quarters the volume of that old copy of *Hawaii*), this book is part travelogue, part chronicle, part natural history, part tell-it-like-it-is, and part encouragement, as it details the concept of "island biogeography"—that islands are most commonly the locale for the extinction of species.

Now I live on a small island. As it turns out, I have lived on islands by choice for a third of my adult life.

I love where I live!

My year abroad as a high school exchange student took me to Honshu, one of the four main islands that make up the country of Japan. (Interestingly, there are over sixty-five-hundred smaller islands that are part of the archipelago of Japan; the smallest size land mass considered an "island" is about three-hundred-twenty-eight feet in circumference.) My host family lived in the far northern part of Honshu in an area considered by Tokyo standards to be "inaka" (countryside); the city I lived in had a quarter of a million residents, so it really didn't feel rural to me. But more than the fact that I was living on an island for what would turn out to be the first of many years of my life, the cultural uniqueness of Japan's island of Honshu is what felt like the biggest adjustment. It wasn't until many years later that I even thought much about that experience as "island living." The sheer size of the island (more than eight hundred miles long) and the fact that it took more than five hours by standard train to travel from Tokyo to Iwate (the prefecture in which I lived that year) were factors that made it seem less island-like to me. I also lived inland, visiting the nearest shoreline—dozens of miles away—perhaps just once that year. Though an incredible experience to live, learn, and study abroad, that year in Japan did not fit my romantic notion of "island living."

Seven years later I found myself living temporarily on an island in the Puget Sound, one that was through and through my "idea" of an island: small enough to bump into coastline in a short drive, treed and verdant, isolated. I had been living and working in Seattle for nearly a year when my mother bought her first house on the island; after decades raising us and living in a place she was finding intolerably crowded and hot, she bought a waterfront cabin on a harbor nestled among isolated, curving island roads. The charm of the place was contagious and in the months between my mom's purchase of the house and moving into it, I stayed there getting some maintenance and remodeling completed before her arrival. Because the job I had in Seattle was structured so that we worked in half-week shifts, I split my time between the island and the city. At the time, I opted to not have a car. So, I would leave work on a Saturday afternoon, board a bus to downtown Seattle, and then another to West Seattle where I could catch the island ferry. I'd board the boat and then take one more bus from the top of the island down to my mom's new home. When I needed groceries, I would wave down and hop on a local island bus, or bring goods with me from the city.

I lived on that same island a second time fifteen years later. The second round of living on the island lasted three years (though I was traveling abroad extensively during that time)—about five times longer than my first residency there. What I realized that second time was that *that* particular island held many challenges for me. Though I had a car the second time, the island is "ferry-locked"; there is no bridge, so any travel off-island requires waiting in the ferry line. The amenities on the island are limited; fewer than ten-thousand people call this island "home" and they have chosen the island for its remoteness, its ruralness. The combination of these factors and others made living on the island too isolating for me; I felt claustrophobic. I was also in a major life transition and had no strong tether to community or work. But by then I was already hanging out on the island I live on now, Bainbridge. I had established a small group of friends, was involved in regular activities (mostly around meditation), and had developed a mad love affair with a particular beach trail on which I ran daily during visits to Bainbridge.

But without much thought at all, and burdened with a fierce need to escape the confines of the island which my mother found so enchanting, I rented a small apartment home and moved from one island to another—from one extreme to another: a remote, bridgeless, and more humble island to a wealthy, amenities-rich place with a bridge on the north end that leads to a network of peninsulas, and a ferry in the center of the island town that leads straight into the heart of downtown Seattle. The island on which I now live is nearly twice as big as the one from which I moved.

Though I haven't circumnavigated our island—as some residents have—on the fifty-three miles of coastline here, I have hiked and walked hundreds of miles on our local beaches. Two particular locations here were my favorites, and where I put the most miles on my feet: one beach on the northeast end of the island and one on the southwest; this was greatly convenient for taking in sunrise and sunset views. After a few years being immersed in island life in the Puget Sound, I realized that I had a deep connection with this region. In a journal entry early one morning, I attempted to capture what has become for me an abiding sense of belonging to this place:

> *The Sound hears my thoughts and safeguards my secrets.*
> *Its ebb and flow continue on day by day mimicking my*
> *own fluctuations. There is a constancy about it. I know*
> *the water will always be there. The sense of permanence,*
> *if only in the scope of my small, mortal life, adds stability*
> *to my core and sustenance for my soul.*

Several years after moving here to this island I call "home," I took a long winter walk with a friend. Upon returning home that day, I wrote the following essay, *Beloved Rain*; it captures my reflections about one of the primary aspects of living in the Pacific Northwest.

Beloved Rain

I sit here in reverence to the rain. It is tenacious. It never seems to empty itself of the liquid healing that also irritates in its persistence. The rain is life giver and sustenance; too, it is metaphor for gloom, darkness, shadow, sadness. In the same moment it offers nourishment to living beings, it is the recipient of derogating taunts. In the same cool breath the rain exhales downward, some humans cry out for heat, light, sun, warmth. The rain cannot provide that. It is rain. Simply the moisture build-up that succumbs to pressure, gravity. Rain heals, opens, nurtures; I will see these gifts if I can remain open.

I recall a few months ago, when the fall had barely given way to winter's frigid air and excessive rain, that a few sane friends were already feeling the boundlessness of the rain; they called it "oppressive." For me, the season had barely begun—I was still really enjoying the rain—and I just wasn't inclined to engage in the darkness of their fever-induced rain mantra: *I can't take it. We've had enough; I need the sun.* But despite my dismay about my friends' rebuke of the natural cycles and beauty that the rain nurtures here in the Pacific Northwest, I found myself similarly crazed within a month of this conversation I had so indignantly judged. Secretly I harbored a grudge against the wall of water that now seemed horizontal rather than vertical. The rain had been falling in train-sized packages (rather than the typical heavy mists or sprinkles), overflowing gutters, and leaking into cement-floor garages. That rain made the ground so sodden it could hold no more; it puddled, pooled, and created ponds in unlikely places. The water was seemingly joined from sky to ground; there was no apparent distinction between that which fell as rain and that which bubbled up into unlikely trenches. The torrent just continued to come and we were inescapably immersed in a seemingly-endless deluge. The unexpected harshness of the rain awakened a brashness within me.

Today as the rain falls, I am softened by remembering that a dear friend is in sorrow; she is experiencing the kind of grief that defies simplicity or tidy wrappings; it is beyond definition itself. In a message meant to soothe her, I carefully straddled the fence between empathy and exhortation: between an honoring of pure, unfixable pain and the vague, empty shell of encouragement. I offered a small (and perhaps shallow) remark about the rain being analogous to tears, and how cleansing salt water is as it flows out eyes and rolls down cheeks.

Yesterday my hospice patient's friends were taking loving, gentle care of her body—offering sweet smelling ointments as balm for her massage-needy skin, making gorgeous gems of their quiet reminiscences to drape around the neck of their dynamic third buddy in a fifty-year trio of companionship. One of them said quietly, "She has a tear." I thought the friend was referring to the discharge that had become more pronounced in the corners of my patient's eyes. But the attending companion said it was rolling down her cheek. Silently, the dying woman offered her own dewy thanks to the friends who tenderly administered the only comfort they knew. There is power in this gesture, huge strength and effort to lie barren of all speech and movement, yet to give the gift of gratitude in one … slow … salty … teardrop.

People who are aware of the Pacific Northwest's reputation as a rainy place, but who do not reside here (and maybe have never visited), will ask: *How can you stand to live in all that rain?* The truth is that it doesn't rain here like it does in other places I've lived or spent lots of time. I recall being a gentle five-year-old sitting near my grandfather in his wheelchair as we'd look out the window counting "one lo-co-mo-tive, two lo-co-mo-tives …" between the lightning and the crashing thunder of New Jersey summer rains; going outside in that torrent would have left my long, brunette braids dripping for the day. During my graduate school years living in New England, I recall the summer rains coming in containers the size of fire trucks. There was no escape from the fragrant soakers; hooded raingear and blowing-inside-out umbrellas were no match for the bounteous rain.

Recently, a friend took me for a walk on the island in order to show me the destruction of some roads, homes, and hillside terraced gardens that had been demolished by a landslide; those excessive rains had loosened the soil around the tree roots causing homes, decks, vegetation, and large trees to crash down in decimating masses of debris. Roads had been closed off, homes evacuated, and everything at the bottom of the hillside lay in rubble and ruins. The homeowners, no doubt, had been lured by the views and proximity to the Sound, if not the price tag, to purchase dwelling places on unstable land. A precipice, sloping sharply and with only loose rocks and turf (that would become gooey mud in the prevalent rain): that was the foundation for these homes. I was struck, incredibly, by the power of water: one drop, two, and then the torrent. Drenching, soaking, uprooting; then felling the exotics in the flower beds, a naturally stained wooden deck, the corner window and wall of somebody's home—all crashing down onto the Lexus of the people whose home below enjoyed a deck overhanging the waters of the high tide.

I cannot help myself but love it; this particular spring day the rain accentuates the crazed green of early spring leaves, the bright yellow blossom on the skunk cabbage, the thirsty mosses on the rock. My appreciation for the gifts of the rain is one response; my utter love of it is another. Sometimes I can appreciate the value of something without particularly *liking* it. Love is from the heart; it just comes unbidden. A moment ago, I hung up the phone from the birthday call to my seventy-six-year-old mother to whom I sent lavender flower photos I had taken, and accompanied by a poem I had written. Her springtime birthday reminds me that life is precious, every drop of rain that falls is a gift, and sometimes a destroyer. What gifts can we find in the rubble of the rain?

About six months later, smack in the center of late spring, I came home from one of my typical hours-long hikes along a stretch of beach here on my island. What follows is the reverie I wrote about it the next morning.

Celebrating Sunny Low Tide

I have lived in a number of beautiful places around this diversely-landscaped country, but none has soothed me with its natural balm like this island in the Pacific Northwest. This verdant rock on which I live measures slightly greater than six by ten miles and is edged by so much coastline; it is considered one of the bigger islands in the Puget Sound region. Our mass is really more water than land with about forty square miles of water on the island; we have an abundance of ponds, lakes, streams, and puddles. It is true that we also have a type of "vertical water mass"; the deluge of rain in winter and the near constant drip the rest of the year create a column of moisture from sea to clouds that is disproportionately favored toward water, too. To have the diversity and abundance of the Crayola-crayon greens that we do, we must learn to live with this excessively high moisture content. Even so, we do have moments in which we must meet our need for the healing light and warmth of the sun.

I keep an eye on the tide chart to see when the waters will be low because I enjoy leisurely walks far and deep along the beach near our home. Two and a half miles down the road there is a state park whose rocky beachfront quickly transitions to one lined with huge houses. If the tide is high or coming in, it is difficult to walk far along that stretch; homeowners' private property and structures encroach close enough to the high tide line to make a beachwalker's journey an arduous one. Trees overhang the beach; boats in various states of disrepair are lined up like children waiting for new clothes; huge logs have piled themselves with the help of waves and tides; and finally, at some point, the salty water abuts the properties. The combination of a sunny warm day *and* low tide in this overcast and rainy Pacific Northwest is a pristine gem. It is impossible to pass up an opportunity to savor this pairing when they come with joined hands. Yesterday was the first such glorious day since winter and I ended up ditching work for a beach walk.

Just minutes after the predicted lowest tide, my exuberant dog and I made our way across the parking lot and grass, toward the water. Stepping up and over the slew of aging rotted logs is part of the journey; they lie parallel to the land and extend for fifty feet onto the beach. My dog loves to sniff everything around those once-trees until she reluctantly heeds my "C'mon!" and joins me farther up the shore. Finding standing pools of saltwater and soft sand beneath her paws, my middle-aged dog began to bound like a puppy. Prancing, jumping, leaping, and running in fast tight circles are her trademarks; my giggles always inspire her to continue her spiraled dashing.

The view at low tide, and on a clear day, is magnificent. "The mountain is out!" we exclaim when we can actually see Mt. Rainier looming to the southeast; sometimes amnesia sets in when we have had too many weeks in a row of gray cloud cover, and the mountain's presence comes as a grand surprise. The mudflats extend down to the low tide line in beautiful textures of taupe wetness. The patterns made from puddles and sand are always refreshing to our eyes and feet on this usually-cobbled rock path. The Cascades lining the eastern horizon were so muted yesterday that only the snow-covered tops were visible, hanging draped from the sky. I paused just after crossing the log piles to search for baby seals who like to lie low on the wet sand during receding tides. A quick scan revealed telltale bumps on the beach, but a closer look disclosed the truth: it was washed up rubbish and large boulders. Still, I stayed alert for movements near or in the water that might indicate pups.

The entire feel of the landscape changes during low tide. The typically rounded textured floor upon which we walk at high tide seems but a fragment of the entire terrain; the sandy beach usually hidden underwater dominated my eyes and my nose yesterday. It is a more fully sensate experience at sunny low tide.

Salted air on my tongue; fishiness in my nostrils; my skin greedily sucking at the sun's warmth; the easier stride on hard packed sand; my occasional stoop to touch the exposed wet sea life; the softer ripple and flow of the long stretches of water saying "Sssh" as they ebb. These sang together in a chorus of sensory delight.

Out in the warmed salty sea breeze, sun stars, anemones, kelp, and eel grass carpeted the tide flats beneath my feet, their usual cover receded for a few hours. I watched, amazed, as a bald eagle flew from his perch atop the snag on the high embankment down to the sand about two hundred feet from where I crouched with my hand in the depression made by a scuttling rock crab. A two-year-old waddled by with the fat neck of a geoduck (also known as "horse neck clams" and "gapers") in her plump, firm grasp; other toddlers in brightly colored bathing suits with sale tags no doubt removed that morning, sat in several inches of pooled water warmed sufficiently to bathtub temperature in the few hours around high noon. I leashed my dog when I noticed a great blue heron standing erect at the water's edge; the tall-legged fisher's long downy chest feathers blew in the breath of the wind as his eyes scanned for a meal. The sand itself seemed to be spewing streams like fireworks; one well-aimed squirt of the clam's saltwater managed to climb the inside of my narrow pant leg. The gulls who joined us on the beach were in search of sustenance; so was I as I filled my cramped body with energizing movement, my soul with glee and beauty.

I am especially grateful now for my decision to take a break in the middle of my work yesterday; the *tinkle-thonk* of water splashing down the insides of the drain pipe as I awoke this morning alerted me to last night's rain before I ever opened my eyes to the droplet covered landscape of my comfortable island dwelling.

A Good Island Life

Island life suits me well. Any excursions off-island (toward Seattle) are dictated by "the boat" and we all have our ferry and wait times memorized for those times of day we most frequently leave the island to go east. And because we have a bridge on the north end of the island, we can plan excursions headed west or sometimes even south with a bit more freedom. I adore the isolation of this place; that is, I adore the combination of isolation and access that our particular island enjoys. Water is a natural boundary offering safety, coziness, and a naturally soothing tidal rhythm. There is a slowing on an island. It's obvious, when the ferry unloads its miles-long string of cars at rush hour, just who lives here and who is merely passing through to cross the north end bridge en route to destinations north or west of our island; passers rush while residents relax. And I always have a choice about whether or not I integrate into "the larger world" (taking the ferry or driving across the bridge); it is of paramount importance to me to know that my haven is a more remote, less peopled one.

Photographs are one of the ways that I document, find the patterns in, and capture the beauty of island life. Every day I see waterscapes, skyscapes, forest trails, and native plants that mesmerize me. What I notice most often as I review (and cull) my burgeoning photograph collection is that I tend to take multiple shots of the water views, particularly if it is dawn or dusk when the light is more rapidly shifting. The combination of the sun on the water, or the clouds backlit by the orb we see less often than folks in more sunny locales, makes my heart sing. My favorite images are the ones in which water and light are in dynamic interplay. I took a photo a few nights ago of the sky and water on a partly cloudy evening. The reflective fusing of cloud and water textures with cerulean, ash, and mercury colors created the sense of a mirror: clouds floating on the water's surface and clouds visible overhead created a kind of containment, holding, safety. I think it is this that I cherish so much as an island resident. On this small hunk of land, I am held by the light on the water and the light in clouds mirroring each other. I am in between. I am caressed by the beauty of edges: water seeps onto beaches and vegetation decays, rolling downhill to create a fertile place for grass and flowers that meet a cobbled shore. Living on an island reminds me how interdependent we are; we rely, neighbor to neighbor, upon one another in a shared identity: residence on the same parcel of Earth. Resident humans. Resident nonhumans.

Island living also cautions me to continue to reach broadly, to engage with the larger world, so that the tendency toward insularity does not move me closer to homogeneity but opens me again and again to the beauty of an entire region, an island continent, an entire island planet in the sea of the cosmos.

Ecological Diversity

SBJ

Henry David Thoreau understood and expressed in *Walden* that we are a component of a grand ecosystem, whether globally or in the neighborhood of the pond. I believe he bemoaned, even then, that man was distancing himself from nature at our species' peril, losing our intelligence with the Earth.

Carl Sagan nailed it. Earth is a pale blue orb, a mote of dust in the vast darkness of space, and to the extent we know, alone. John McPhee observed in *Basin and Range* that if we stand, extending arms horizontally, one to each side, representing with them the entire sweep of Earth's 4.5 billion years, one strike of a medium-grained fingernail file across the nail of the extended present hand finger would erase all of human history. I offer this context as a reminder. Recently I walked a friend's 90-acre property. We talked boldly of native and non-native species and of invasive exotics. How odd and how arrogant for us to think that anything from this tiny isolated planet could be termed foreign, out of place, alien, invasive, not belonging, or disruptive.

Jennifer J. Wilhoit, Ph.D. and Stephen B. Jones, Ph.D.

A Forester's Perspective

Long ago, as an entry-level industrial forester, I spoke of forest *stands* as though they were sacrosanct, contained, site-partitioned units of forest similar in age, species composition, structure, and site quality. Their component tree, shrub, and herbaceous vegetation, in part, defined the limits and bounds, and helped determine management prescriptions. Within-stand and between-stand diversity guided me as I decided what treatments to prescribe. One might ask what it means to prescribe *treatments* and why we should tamper with forests that have done quite well without us for far longer than we, as a species, have been walking upright. A simple response is that we require food, water, habitat, shelter, air, beauty, and recreation at levels beyond what the natural, unmanaged floral and faunal communities (ecosystems) of Earth can furnish. Forest ecosystems cover approximately 30 percent of terrestrial Earth, a little less than 10 percent of the Earth's total surface, water included.

So, we must prescribe and impose *treatments* to modify forest composition (tree species), density (stems per acre), fertility, competition, and select other elements. We need not do this on all forests, yet we were certainly so inclined on the bulk of the 1.7 million acres my employer-company owned during the 12 years of my employment (1973-1985). As the company's Alabama Woodlands Region Land Manager (1981-85), I held direct responsibility for managing 320,000 acres (500 square miles) of some of the most productive forestland in the South. We did not permit nature to run her course. We guided and directed those natural systems. Although we strove to optimize long-term economic return and furnish the raw material for paper and allied products manufacturing, we did so with reverence for the land and the community of life within our forests. We protected waterways; preserved rare, threatened, and endangered species (e.g., red-cockaded woodpecker and gopher tortoise) and their requisite habitats; and practiced on the basis of long-term sustainable yield of forest goods and services. I wrote the company's formal Forest Practices Manual in 1981. I can vouch for the company's devotion to a land ethic. We were in it for the long haul.

Just as we feed the world effectively by dedicating production on single crop species (soybean, corn, sugar beets, etc.) at an industrial scale, so must we concentrate forest production via intensive silvicultural treatments on land well-suited to such focused and intentional management. Nearly eight billion people consume unfathomable quantities of food, wood, water, shelter. As the standard of living elevates over the intervening population growth years, 11 billion will consume far greater than 50 percent more than we do now. We have an essential obligation to produce and extract such goods and services responsibly and sustainably, sensitive to the impacts and consequences near-term, and centuries hence. Our awareness and responsibility extend to a basic ecosystem foundation, the diversity and richness of life on Earth, globally and at the site and micro-site levels.

Ecological Richness

The term diversity—whether in biological, social, corporate, legislative, or political settings—has risen to near-exalted status: a single, dominant attribute that seems to shine more brightly and carries more weight than all other variables combined. Think of what some might view as the terribly myopic decision that led the Civilian Conservation Corps (CCC) in the 1930s to plant pure stands of red, white, or Scots pine on tens of thousands of acres across the central Appalachians. However, from my perspective, the reforestation imperative superseded any concern about creating a monoculture of a single tree species.

Instead, I picture tens of thousands of acres abused by over-grazing and ruinous tillage that the CCC efforts reclaimed from the ravages of water and gravity. The stands of a single tree species held the soil in place and restored vast acreages, now supporting forests of deep beauty, magic, and wonder. CCC-planted white pine forests near Asheville's Biltmore Estate served as the opening (*primeval* forest) chase scene for the late twentieth century *Last of the Mohicans* movie. Magnificent towering white pine, a forest cathedral flourishing with trees, shrubs, and herbaceous vegetation, all elements acting interdependently, and effectively holding the worn-out, abandoned, agricultural soils in place as intended, with results far beyond even the hopeful expectations of CCC visionaries.

To all but the practiced eye, the stand *is* the forest primeval! So, not such a bad decision after all to plant the eroded land with a single native species! As we hear in medicine, first, do no harm. Some 80 years ago, the CCC practiced triage, stopped the bleeding (severe soil erosion) by first ceasing steep hillside row cropping and overgrazing; connected the IV (planted white pine seedlings); and provided long-term care (protection from fire and grazing). Time then did its magic, in concert with nature's insistence on tolerating no vacuum. Wind- and animal- disseminated seed gradually brought diversity to the so-called white pine *monoculture*.

Over the past few months I've visited two distinctly different wilderness areas: the Sipsey in west-central Alabama and Dolly Sods in West Virginia's northern highlands. Far different geology, climate, substrate, vegetation, past use (yes, both wilderness areas saw extensive attempts by settlers at domestication), and ecological destiny. Each has its own range of diversity within, unique collections of natural communities. A richness "untrammeled by man, where man himself is a visitor who does not remain." Yet on each I saw some *exotics* and *invasives*. Plants, that is. We have no way of knowing how many foreign insects slipped through the wilderness boundary. To my knowledge, all *alien* invaders came from well within Earth's home ecosystem. The Earth is a self-contained ecosystem, whose habitable boundaries are defined by extremes of climate, and by little else. The Sahara Desert, Antarctic icescapes, the Himalayas, and other such unfriendly climatic zones limited and constrained life and floral and faunal colonization by exotics and invasives. All other more habitable locations are open to natives and non-natives alike.

Purists among my fellow plant scientists are adamant that those invasive interlopers do not enrich the wilderness biotic community by adding diversity. They believe that such exotics foul the natural environment. Yet, I struggle reconciling that if diversity is good, pure, and oh-so-important to internal balance, resilience, power, beauty, wonder, magic, performance, and ecosystem function, then *introduced* diversity is bad.

I've done a little international travel: including dense and deep immersion across North America, and more superficially in Scandinavia,

Europe, and Asia. Strange lands, yes, but rich with trees, shrubs, and herbaceous plants very familiar to me, at least at the genus level. No wonder. Super-continent Pangaea encompassed nearly all terrestrial crustal plates for eons, until beginning to separate 175 million years ago. Again, we exalt *diversity*, yet abhor kudzu's release to Georgia and Alabama and the chestnut blight and Dutch elm disease infecting American chestnut and American elm. We are so human-centric (our biases seem aligned with things that we humans enjoy, use, admire, get sentimental about) with respect to our prejudices about exotics and invasives. I suppose we might welcome a red maple seedling dug from a sandy roadside in northern Florida and transplanted to a similarly sandy, glacial outwash roadside in Ontario. After all, both are native to North America. Although both individuals are of the same species, I suspect that genotype (differences among species that are genetically induced) differs enough that neither will thrive, and may not survive, transplanted to the other's home.

We *Homo sapiens* are more similar to each other than any one of us is to all other living organisms on the planet. Among us, we are diverse in culture, values, place of origin, life experience, learning, religion, and so many other characteristics, yet we are one. You certainly wouldn't know it from sampling the news. I puzzle over how differences (diversity) can both spawn such pervasive acrimony and violence, and yet rise to near deity status in our modern culture. It seems a paradox that diversity can be conditionally both so good and so abhorrent.

Diversity as a Tool

I am not a genuine handyman, yet I do have a tool chest. Thirteen interstate moves taught me that man does not live by hammer, pliers, and flat blade screwdriver alone. I can handle almost any picture-hanging, curtain and blind installation, and door hinge adjustment. I have enough diversity in my tool kit to manage the tasks that do not exceed my wisdom, knowledge, experience, and ability. I know guys with a garage full of power tools and "big boy toys." Some of these guys actually know how to use them, and do, drawing great admiration and accolades from me. However, I have a phone, and can generally achieve similar end results. Doing it themselves gives great satisfaction and fulfillment to these friends. Trying to reach beyond my handy-man grasp gives me headaches, shortness of breath, damaged goods, and an eventual call to the same vendor who would then cost me more after I messed up things! For me, the option that gets it done is better. I don't need to be handy-man self-sufficient. I just want the lawnmower to cut the grass, the garage door to open and close, and the refrigerator to keep dispensing ice. I'd rather observe nature, and learn her lessons, mechanical contrivances be damned! I don't even like washing my car, much less rebuilding the engine!

So, some might suggest that full-breadth diversity, whether in the garage, the business leadership team, or in the forest stand, is necessary, beneficial, and the ultimate aim. I am not of that absolute mind. There is cost in diversity being a desired end. There is considerable cost, for example, in reduced return on investment, for having your own acetylene torch and welding gear. Or for managing every forest unit to support all major central Appalachian hardwood species. The responsible forester will question the purpose of such full species diversity. An informed forester will see stand composition as a tool for achieving an outcome, whether it be forest products, wildlife management, water protection and yield, aesthetics, recreation, or peace of mind.

I rebel against the notion of diversity just for the sake of diversity. What I want in a leadership team, whether my own at one of the universities I've led as CEO, or for our leaders in Washington, operates along lines I can compile:

- Character – honesty, integrity, trustworthiness, commitment, hard work, professional ethics, service orientation, good humor, a belief in something larger and more lasting
- Future orientation, shared mission, common cause
- Work ethic
- Embrace of Earth stewardship
- Diversity of geographic experiences, cultural immersions, career exposures

I start running out of gas if and when attributes like age, sex, race, sexual orientation, and other factors begin muscling the items above from preeminence.

With respect to leading a university, I seek results. My teams have comprised just a single species. I am less concerned with checking a series of arbitrary input boxes (gender, national origin, etc.) and much more focused on checking a full list of results boxes. Importantly, all of our faculty, staff, students, alumni, supporters, partners, donors, and community members are *Homo sapiens*, residents of this mote of dust.

Each and every forest stand on our pale blue orb comprises multiple species. Even a post-fire, clonal-derived aspen stand covering multiple acres in Alaska's interior, is rich with invading birch, willow, and understory vegetation. Every natural system and all socio-economic human enterprises feel the tremendous, unyielding, relentless force of eons. Time is nothing to the cosmos, and not of much consequence to Mother Earth.

Time is everything to us human inhabitants. I fear we may be traveling at sixty minutes per hour toward our own demise. I believe that focusing on some level of designated diversity cannot save us from our destiny. In fact, our Earth is blessed with grand and ubiquitous diversity, across geography and previously over the vast sweep of time since life emerged on Earth. This life-rich globe has sustained catastrophic asteroid impacts, the calamitous emergence of green plants that *poisoned* the atmosphere with oxygen, and cataclysmic volcanic eruptions. I truly wonder if it can handle a so-called *advanced* species running amok.

We must be *advanced* enough to first delay, and then prevent our seeming self-imposed peril. Judy and I have sowed plant seed each spring for 47 years. Not all germinate and not all germinants survive. In some ways, we humans represent a trial garden, seeded by a higher hand or perhaps by the chance of evolution. We may be a freak of nature, a chance flicker here in a distant arm of our home galaxy, destined to flame and fade across time and distance that know no bounds. Judy and I will leave behind two kids and five grandchildren, and they, too, we pray, will extend the reach further. Perhaps on and on until we as a species learn what is truly critical.

Yes, ecological diversity is significant, yet it is important only in terms of human intervention and impact, only in terms of our human needs to extract and use products, goods, services, and amenities from nature. Without humans, natural systems will remain rich, robust, viable, vibrant, and sustainable, until the next asteroid or other cataclysmic event. And then Earth's natural systems will adjust, and then flourish as they shift to yet another derived global ecological variant. Like it or not, *Homo sapiens* is part of today's natural equation. I do not purport to know what constitutes, or how to achieve, some optimum level of ecological diversity on Earth.

Nature does not seek some diversity target. Instead, natural systems diversify and expand by filling all ecological niches. When perturbations occur, some niche occupants are positioned to fill disturbance-voids. Change, adaptation, and exploitation will allow no void to remain empty for long. Recall again that nature abhors a vacuum.

Yes, I retain fidelity to my contention that nature offers countless lessons for life and living. Yet I am not ardently and unconditionally waving the flag for diversity. Don't misinterpret me. I am a diversity proponent. Just not for the sole sake of diversity itself. Instead, let's view diversity in life, business, and service as an assurance. An investment in being prepared for operating contingencies: not all possible contingencies, just for those that are likely. Diversity can bring strength. Diversity for its own sake can dilute and weaken, if that diversity is secured at the price of yielding strengths, competence, and depth where it is most needed.

Nature doesn't generally find distraction in shiny objects. Ecological diversity stands as an important concept, one we must understand and appreciate. Yet it is not the end-all. Likewise, social, economic, and cultural diversity is important, but it is not the end. Instead, diversity is just one means that may be critical in achieving a desired result.

As Muir noted, we and every element of Earth's ecosystem are hitched to everything else in the universe. We clearly do not know all we need to understand about the dense web of interconnectivity. And we do not comprehend the thresholds of impact and consequence that our actions, intended and otherwise, have on the one great global ecosystem that sustains *Homo sapiens*. I fear that we are uncertain whether we are plunging headlong into an abyss of our own making. We need to know where the ecosystem resilience and ecological impact lines cross, teetering us over some unanticipated threshold. Ecological diversity is a central buffer to catastrophe, yet ecological diversity suffers consequentially from our expanding human population and exploding consumption of land, goods, and services.

Henry David Thoreau spent his 26 months at Walden Pond some 170 years ago. In *Walden*, he wrote, "Shall I not have intelligence with the Earth? Am I not partly leaves and vegetable mould myself? What is the pill that will keep us well, serene, contented? Not my or thy great-grandfather's, but our great-grandmother Nature's universal, vegetable, botanic medicines, by which she has kept herself young always…" He understood that we are a component of that grand ecosystem, whether globally or in the neighborhood of the pond. I believe he bemoaned, even then, that man was distancing himself from nature at our species' peril, losing our "intelligence with the Earth." He spoke with unqualified reverence for the richness of life around Walden Pond.

I believe, in my heart of hearts, that we can reawaken the passion and wisdom that Muir and Thoreau felt and expressed. We are, and we must be, capable of recognizing and preserving the ecosystem richness that sustains us. My own mission relates intimately to the cause Muir and Thoreau embraced implicitly: "Employ writing and speaking to educate, inspire, and enable readers and listeners to understand, appreciate, and enjoy Nature, and accept and practice Earth stewardship." Sustaining our Earth ecosystem and maintaining ecological diversity are central to ensuring our future as global citizens.

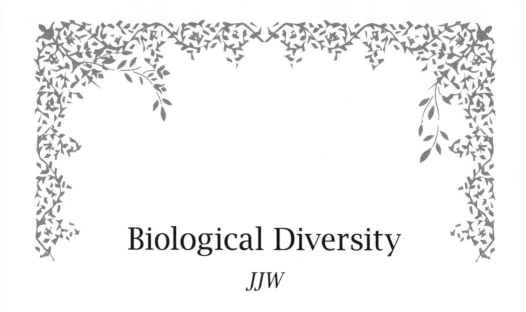

Biological Diversity

JJW

Biological diversity is the variety of life in the
world or in a particular habitat or ecosystem.

We live on this incredibly beautiful, spinning planet that is rushing
headlong through infinite space. The bones of this orb are made of
fire and rock. The Earth's epidermis is liquid: the salty seas of this
sumptuous sphere with swimming beings as large as blue whales,
crawling ones like crabs and turtles, invertebrates (corals, anemones,
jellyfish) of amazing shapes and textures. Or the freshwater lakes, bogs,
and rivers. In other places, our home's surface skin is soil, teeming with
tiny creatures—some only discernible through microscopes. Atop this
grow the redwoods and rhododendrons, sagebrush and sword fern; and
on some of these living beings grow other beings: mosses, lichens, ivy,
mushrooms. We cannot forget, either, the vast stretches of sandy places
and rocky spots that we call by names like "Mojave" and "Kalahari."
And awash upon us at any moment are raindrops or snow, great gushing
breezes, thick sheets of hot sunlight, or columns of fog. We gaze up to
view the sun or moon, planets and stars, clouds forming and re-forming,
a firmament bluer than blue, colors at sun risings or sunsets.

I have seen a sampling of the jaw-dropping ecological diversity on
all seven continents of this great Earth. In the way that much of my

life has unfolded (a mix of serendipity, divine intervention, following my intuition, heartfelt passion, and enthusiastic efforts to accomplish scholarly and personal goals), I never planned or set out to see every continent on the planet. It was only in my early middle-age that I even heard of people ticking off one land mass after another, upon returning from travel abroad, in an attempt to be a "Seven Continent-er." I just accepted opportunities that were offered and reached for others that I found compelling. And at the age of forty-eight, I placed my palms face down on my seventh continent. The overwhelming unbelievability of the ecological diversity of this sphere we call "Home" cannot be overstated. My mother suggested for years that I write a book about the adventures I have had while traveling; this never occurred to me to be something of great interest—to me or to my readership. Plenty of people have covered that territory already; books abound about adventures large and small on just about every square mile of the world. But this essay beckons me to share a word-snapshot per continent in order to emphasize the personal blessings that this Earth's biodiversity has to offer. Simple engagement, potent impact. Pure presence in a moment, a lifetime of appreciation.

Asia

My first experience in Asia was during my junior and senior years in high school. After a series of intensive interviews by the program, I had been selected as an exchange student to spend a year in Japan. Because I had checked off "anywhere" on the list of places I was willing to go, I figured I would be sent to a place that other teenage exchange students didn't find ideal: an off-the-grid hut somewhere very remote. Instead, I was totally surprised that the program leaders felt Japan was a good match for my sensitivities and adaptability. That year was a formative one during which I became conversant in Japanese, attended the local high school, and lived with a traditional Japanese family. I'm not sure if my love of genteel Asian cultures came from that year abroad or not. But since then I have traveled to a host of countries in East Asia including: Sulawesi, China, Thailand, Nepal, and Myanmar (Burma). Seeing the amazing and vast biodiversity in Indonesia; pandas in China; dolphins, crocodiles, and riverscapes in Nepal; and birds I will never be able to name in Thailand, opened my eyes to worlds beyond worlds of nature's incredible varieties and adaptations.

I went to Burma a couple of times to do graduate research. I was both an ecotourist assisting with two cetacean scientists' research on river dolphins, as well as a principal investigator conducting my own Master's research on intercultural, environmental group learning. During our time abroad, we lived on and conducted our research aboard a cramped riverboat on the Irrawaddy River. These tiny quarters made stops in the villages very desirable to us; it was an opportunity to stretch our legs, swim in the cool water, and learn about local culture. From the moment I landed the first time in Myanmar, I was seduced by the sweet generosity of the Burmese people. The tropical landscape held me in bliss as I journeyed through teak forests, gilded temples, villages loaded with bamboo huts on stilts, and along riverbanks overcrowded with fishermen, women panning for gold, families bathing and laundering, animals drinking.

The second time I was in Burma, I had a more intensive experience with the cetologists' research which was focused on the cooperative fishing phenomenon between local fishermen and the Irrawaddy dolphin. We wanted to understand more about the local human-dolphin relationship, the lore that was described to us in the villages and alongside the river. By making dawn to dusk observations and recordings of human and dolphin activity, we were able to verify the stories we had been told. I saw this cooperation happen. Local men in canoes tapped their particular rhythm onto the boat's edge using a "*labai* call": a carved wooden implement about the size of a hammer and the shape of a tapered bat. The dolphins actually responded to certain of the fishermen, and when they "trusted" the particular fisher, they would form as a group and curve their bodies to herd schools of fish into the area where the fishermen were to cast their round nets. Each time this resulted in a huge catch for the fisherman and his young son, as well as a feast for the dolphins who scooped up the mass of fish that surged into their mouths as the net was pulled from the water. Never before in my life had I been a firsthand witness to such a mutually beneficial and cooperative endeavor between nonhumans and humans.

Africa

On a study trip to Egypt during my graduate years, I was thrilled to be making my first excursion to the African continent. And I was completely intrigued with the seemingly featureless sand of the Sahara Desert (through which we traveled for days by bus to get to an oasis). On one of the many breaks from driving, I found myself outside taking stock of the former seabed of the Sahara. Squatting down to peer more closely—like a mirage, except real when I picked it up—was a seashell or, rather, a fossilized seashell. The swirling imprint of an ocean that had vanished too long ago to be believed. A seabed that was the complete opposite of the desiccated landscape through which we journeyed. There is nothing like three days of travel through the solely-sand landscape of that vast desert to teach a traveler the vital necessity of water, the meaning of mirage, the value of oasis.

On another trip many years later, I visited South Africa and had the opportunity to camp with a local guide in Kruger National Park; we fell asleep to the snorting and howls of rhinoceroses and awoke to the screams of monkeys. Painted dogs—as wild as the canid comes, birds of every shape and size and color, the Big Five (lion, leopard, rhino, elephant, and buffalo), zebras and elephants and giraffes in numbers shocking to the casual American zoo-goer, and so many more creatures I have no names for created one of the most species-rich experiences I have ever had.

But my weeks in Rwanda conducting field research for my dissertation stand out as the most remarkable of my travels in Africa, perhaps simply because I spent so much time there. Each day I would trek twenty-five-hundred feet down a steep and pine-needles-slippery mountain into a small village where I did my research. The women (and a few men) who lived in that remote village had agreed to talk to me about their crafts coop, formed as an economic boost after the genocide events in the early 1990s. The artisans had a generations-long tradition of weaving baskets from a local, grass-like weed. But they had been encouraged by foreigners to expand their crafts to include images of the local flora and fauna. Women were learning how to draw colobus monkeys, for example, on colored cotton cloth, and then stitching the outlined figures with appropriate (fur-colored) thread. What stunned me every day was not just the tenacity of these women, but the fact that they lived in such a remarkably beautiful place. The cloud forest of their corner of the country was the densest I've ever seen. And the sounds of creatures large and small who moved and called, cried and stomped through those forests in the middle of the night were enough to keep me vigilant as I stayed all alone in a room in the forest at the top of the mountain above the artisans' village.

Each of these three very unique places on the African continent offered me a breadth of vision about the incredible ecological diversity that inhabits our amazing planet.

Europe

I first went to Europe when I was nineteen years old; I was taking a "gap-year"—though that term was not in use then. I had worked hard to save for a fancy SLR camera, down sleeping bag, and a sojourner's backpack. I spent six weeks mostly staying with relatives of my mom's best friend in Germany, seeing more incredibly beautiful castles than I ever knew existed. Other times I flew through Europe en route to more distant locales in Africa; on one such layover I drank beer in a pub in an outskirt of London and on another one I ate Belgian chocolate that made my African-borne intestinal parasites roll over one another as I flew the final leg of the journey home. But those early trips did not provide much opportunity for a deeper look at natural landscapes.

Twenty years later, during an anguishing impasse in my doctoral progress, I took a trip to Scotland with my mother. We had traveled together prior to then, vacations we called "painting tours." We decided the remote Shetland Islands (geographically closer to Norway than Scotland) would be an inspirational spot for our creative efforts. My artist mother and I carried our art supplies with us and found outdoor places in which we would spend the morning painting. We went sightseeing in the towns and countryside in the afternoons. What I most remember about the natural history of the Shetlands was its starkness! The open landscape—so different from the tall, dense forests of my beloved Pacific Northwest, or of the thick underbrush and close trunks in the stands of trees in my then-residence in New England—startled me. Moors with hardly a tree in sight. Modern white windmills, monoliths on the otherwise featureless hilltops. And the broad stretch of July daylight that seemed relentless and made me restless; at two in the morning dusk finally settled in until first light appeared through the curtains around four. These wee hours of wakefulness especially fed my angst about my doctoral research.

I found that the natural landscape of the North Shetland Islands directly "mirrored" my inner struggle (to make sense of my research data). At a distance, the Shetlands' landscape appeared almost featureless. But at close range (an encounter with a wild pony who nuzzled us through the car window, the tiny hillside flowers that were only visible if I got on the ground on my hands and knees, the up-close textures of grasses), the incredible diversity and richness of the island became apparent. Likewise, with my doctoral research, I first saw a vast, dry mass of incomprehensible information: this was the impasse (an inability to make sense of my data) I found myself in during the Shetlands trip. But upon returning home I took a closer look at the data and saw beautiful, intricate details that led to theoretical insights and (a few months later) a cohesive dissertation. What I experienced as the starkness of the Shetlands at a landscape scale became lushness at the level of flora and fauna; what seemed barren and simplistic in my uncompiled doctoral research became bountiful insight at the level of themed data.

North America

I have traveled all over this continent on which I live. And I have lived on both the east and west coasts, as well as a short drive from the continental divide for a few years. On multiple occasions I have driven back and forth across the United States, including one summer during which I did a graduate research project covering more than ten thousand miles and seven national parks in four weeks. I've made excursions up and down both coasts and traveled inland routes repeatedly. The summer before my thirtieth birthday I rode more than sixteen hundred miles on my bicycle, zigzagging in and out of rainforests, beaches, forests, and the hilly terrain of the Pacific Coast. I have even done a number of multiple-day fasts in wilderness areas for spiritual growth and insight. In all of these journeys I have encountered wildlife, the wild outback, landscapes, and weather that stun, elate, induce fear, and pacify me. A mounting summer tornado that grew and formed and touched the ground then receded before my very eyes, rising back up with clouds of dust in its funnel. A cougar on a hillside near the road I traveled in my car: staring at me, watching me. Lightning so close it raised my long hair above my head to utterly vertical.

But about ten years ago, I had the rare opportunity to stroke a newborn gray whale in the calving lagoons in Baja. I also had extended physical contact with the mama gray who stayed alongside the Zodiak for nearly thirty minutes; she then nudged her baby up against our rubber raft, apparently not perceiving us as a threat. The prolonged engagement with these phenomenal creatures in their "nursery" was a highlight among the many North American travels and natural-world encounters I've experienced. I was simultaneously giggling and crying in the moments of physical contact: leaning across the top of the inflated vessel so that only the tip of my toe wedged under a handle kept me inside the boat, I stretched out and stroked that mama and her baby, over and over again. I talked to her in whispers so the other passengers couldn't hear my love stories. I looked her in the eye—that massive organ just inches from my face—and I strained to rest my head alongside her slick wet hulk. I was told later about some of the jovial things other passengers were saying, about the photos that were taken of those whales and me from nearby boats, about the unprecedented experience I had been gifted. But at the time of my encounter, all I knew was gray, gray whale, mama, baby, wetness, the spray of her exhale wetting my hair and face over and over again.

South America

South America is the continent I have explored the least. I feel like I should have spent more time there: because it is so close to my own homeplace; because I have a number of South American friends from several of the countries on that huge mass of land; and because so many of my family members, friends, and colleagues have spent considerable time traveling to, living in, doing ecological research there.

That said, I have been to a limited area in Argentina five or six times and passed through Chile once on a flight layover. My route in Argentina was always the same: fly into the international airport in Buenos Aires, take a taxi across the city to the national airport, and fly down to "The End of the World"—Ushuaia, a precious port city at the southern tip of Argentina. This is the point of departure for ships carrying North and South American visitors to Antarctica. The Beagle Channel is the close edge of the dreaded Drake Passage—that swirling, tumultuous, infamous waterway between South America and the Antarctic peninsula.

My stays in Ushuaia have been punctuated by the beauty of the Tierra del Fuego region. The city sits nestled along a slope of the Andes Mountains and I have hiked in this area just once outside of the city. I happened to be very sick with a pre-walking pneumonia condition developing. But the scheduled hike was my only opportunity to get out of the city and into the incredibly lush landscape I could only barely see from sea level. It enticed and called me. So, though I was very sick, and came down off the mountain that day with quite a fever, I hiked up the steep slope to views of lakes, forests, and a moorlike area that contained low shrubs and open space. It was like a dream. In fact, I mean this literally. About eleven years prior, I had dreamt of an emerald green mountainscape that seemed to hold surprises and gems, mysteries and intrigue.

The crystalline image of that dream stayed with me for years. It was over a decade later as I hiked in that mountaintop area above the city of Ushuaia that I had the déjà vu that took me back to a sleepy night in my early thirties. The dream (of my sleep) became the dream that I lived that day hiking, feverish, in the teal azure mountains at the tip of the world.

Jennifer J. Wilhoit, Ph.D. and Stephen B. Jones, Ph.D.

Australia

Seven years ago, I submitted a proposal to present my work at a professional conference focused on environmental sustainability. One of several major enticements for me was that the conference was being held in Canberra, Australia. This would be my "seventh continent." But I would only go if my proposal were accepted. I could not afford to travel that distance without justification. Months went by and I forgot all about the proposal. Then the acceptance letter came and I was thrilled! Even as I prepared professionally and personally for the conference and trip, I became inordinately focused on seeing a koala. I knew that I wouldn't probably just come across a koala sitting under a eucalyptus tree as I walked through Sydney or Canberra, my two destinations of the trip.

Shortly after I arrived in Sydney, I located a wildlife refuge a few hours from the city. I made a mental note to figure out the logistics at the end of my trip when I'd have thirty-six hours back in Sydney before boarding the plane home. The mostly-rural train ride between Sydney and Canberra was beautiful and interesting, but—of course—I did not see kangaroos and koalas running through the landscape. The conference was an incredibly empowering experience and was the first time I began to realize how interdisciplinary, integrated, and crucial my new business was in the larger scheme of things: sustainability, spiritual ecology, personal renewal. Back in Sydney, I followed up on my promise to myself and paid attention to my intuition. A B&B owner had loudly rejected my plan to go to the particular wildlife refuge I'd selected, urging me to visit the nearby zoo instead. I just couldn't do it. I politely thanked her and proceeded with determining the details for transportation to the distant wildlife center, at least a three-hour journey each way.

For some reason, many of the trains were not running that day, I had not rented a car (preferring to travel by foot whenever possible), and I only had an eight-hour window in which to make the trek. I could not afford any delays or missed transports in that narrow timeframe. Finding my way in a totally new place is not my forte. But by some miracle of alternate trains and buses—and allowing myself to carry the angst and real possibility of getting totally lost or never making it to the refuge—I wound through the city, suburbia, and then a rural countryside to the refuge. I was the only person on the bus, and the stop for the refuge was not marked; by total serendipity I got off the bus in the right spot and wandered on back roads until I saw a small sign pointing toward the refuge. Somehow I had made it, and I was ecstatic with this feat even before I walked through the refuge gate.

Once inside I quickly became acquainted with a host of species I'd never met before, some with names totally unfamiliar to me. I watched some of the presentations by wildlife conservationists. I roamed past every enclosure of mammals, birds, and tree species they had highlighted. I even spent a good long while with mature and newborn kangaroos, enjoying the lack of restrictions on distance from or touching of the animals; I petted, talked to, followed, and observed the kangas. I laughed like a child when the kangaroo touched me with his arm. My first stop had been to the koala enclosure and I had seen a few of the sleeping fur balls hanging out in the trees, seemingly precariously perched as if a snore might knock them out of the branches and onto the ground thirty feet below.

But I needed a more intimate encounter. I heard that a naturalist would hold a koala close to the audience and talk about its biology during a formal presentation. I was there ten minutes early. Apparently, my enthusiasm was written across my face in a wide smile throughout the informative talk. Afterward, the other visitors immediately filed off to different exhibits, but the kind biologist quietly whispered that I should stay. She held the koala within my reach and began to answer my incessant questions. This chance to spend extended time with a koala in a refuge outside of Sydney, Australia was nothing short of sheer romance. Holding, hugging, talking to, observing, and even kissing this koala on the shoulder was *the* experience that truly *made* my work trip to Australia. Ten minutes in close proximity to a wild creature can be transformative. The long and unsure journey to briefly meet a single koala—to touch and engage with him—was absolutely one worth undertaking.

Antarctica

I was determined to abide by all of the regulations we had been briefed about aboard ship. The Antarctic Treaty lays out some very specific guidelines about many facets of journeying through the coldest, windiest, driest continent on Earth. The distance one is admonished to keep from wildlife is just but one of these crucial rules. I would not be going an inch closer than the prescribed distance to any penguin, seal, avian.

What follows in italics is just one of the many profound, *in-the-moment* engagements I had with wildlife near the Antarctic peninsula over the course of half a dozen journeys to the southernmost region of our planet.

I see a few, and then a dozen, and then suddenly a whole beachful of baby elephant seals, affectionately called "weaners," as they have just stopped being nourished by their mothers. They are lumbering up onto land out of the frigid southern Atlantic Ocean. Suddenly and irrevocably I am struck with a powerful affection for these creatures. They are nothing like me at all, and yet I feel sure I could communicate something of this lovestruckness if I could just get close enough. But I will abide by the strict rules that have been detailed for us. As one of the only passengers (of the one hundred and ninety-nine aboard ship) to have done any formal graduate work in environmental studies, I am even more determined to uphold an ethical standard that is exemplary. It is just about more than I can tolerate though. I know these babies have spent their first few weeks solely in the care of a mama of their own species, but I want to lavish them with tender motherly affection of a human sort: petting their thick, as-yet-unmarred hides; offering a hand for their olfactory perusal; and to kiss them on the tops of their wrinkled foreheads. Yes, kiss them.

I do not tend to be germ-phobic nor averse to the detritus or "uncleanliness" (per human standards) of wild outdoor creatures. Nor did I fear any type of aggression or other negative response from these newborns. My tolerance for getting dirty from interaction with other creatures—"goo" on my clothes or bare skin—has always been high. But none of this was going through my head as I watched the adorable, roly-poly weaners approaching; I was ready to engage at whatever level some weaner might choose. After all, in the scant few weeks that the weaners had been alive on the planet, they had never been exposed to human beings. And as they matured, they would not have continual exposure to *Homo sapiens*.

But I am far from the cobbled tideline where these babies are congregating. I have chosen to be deeper back on the beach, away from the sounds of my fellow humans who have also traveled long and far to get to this remote island. I want to savor the views, linger in silence. But then I see that a few of the babies are making their slow-going way in my direction. Every few feet they are distracted by one thing or another and it's inconceivable to me that they will ever bother to drag themselves this far away from the abundant curiosities at the water line. I long to crawl belly to pebbles, legs outstretched and elbows reaching forward in small strides, to arrive nose to nose with one of these weaners. These babies weigh almost as much as I do. Their innocence is palpable.

Suddenly, I realize that one baby is actually heading directly toward me. Four yards, then three. Six feet, and then a breath-holdingly-close four feet. I'm sitting in a half-squatting position, black ship-issued rubber boot sticking out in front of my knee. This baby elephant seal has now approached much closer than I would've been allowed to do, but we are not required to move away from the seals if they enter into the space that we humans are required to keep. So I hold my breath and try to suppress audible laughter. And now the baby is nosing my black rubber boot ... rubbing up against it, and then my knee. I hold very still, almost frozen, except for the sharp breaths and uncontrollable smile that are now taking over my entire corpus. Nothing else exists in this moment except the weaner's huge, black, glassy eyes fixed on mine. He nudges closer and puts his mouth on my knee ... then my chest, my neck. He is climbing forward and his chest is now resting on my knee. I know I am not supposed to touch him (per those wildlife rules), but I have now lost track of any notion of right and wrong, and the back of my left hand rubs his belly. (I can confirm this in photographs someone took of my encounter with the weaner.) As I feel his wet, slippery skin on the hand that is petting him, his closed muzzle reaches forward a bit more and gently touches my chin. And now his mouth is on my lips, on my cheek, until finally he makes a deep nudge and places his entire muzzle on my left eye and forehead. All the while his eyes are open—just an inch from my own.

Those several minutes of very intimate contact with a species so unlike me, in such an unlikely place, indelibly marked me. It was an unexpected bliss.

Daily Diversity

These incredible experiences in this chapter have been life altering—some in their singularity, and all of them in sum total. But I do not believe it takes these once-in-a-lifetime encounters to really know and appreciate this Earth on which we live and breathe. I have spent many, many years going outside on a daily basis and touching the soil in my back yard. Watching the birds in the various places I have lived. Studying geography, experiencing different types of weather, becoming familiar with the flora and fauna that share a particular landscape. And it is this regular, ordinary, everyday engagement that I know can bring us into perfect alignment with the bounty of the natural world, and the bounty within ourselves. The hallmark trips and travels can fade over time, become altered—diminished or augmented—by memory. But the observations and encounters we can have, the learning and intimacy that result from that over time in a particular location are the real stuff of connection with Earth. Despite all of these lifechanging moments, the sustained change takes place within me *each* and *every* day.

As I drafted this chapter through many iterations over weeks, I watched the goings-on across the little patch of land that I can see from my desk window. Most especially, perhaps because it was springtime during the writing of this chapter, I paid close attention to the particular bird species who has captured my attention over and over again here in the Pacific Northwest: the dark-eyed junco. Resident, native, compelling. One night I wrote:

> *The junco nest that two adult birds built in my flower basket three and a half weeks ago is full of activity. It hangs just outside my kitchen window, so I have a way of observing them that goes unnoticed and keeps my passionate curiosity from interfering with their progress.*

I climb up a step stool and onto the kitchen counter. Through miniblinds that I've shut to keep our movements in the house from disturbing the ever-watchful, protective parents, I can peek to see the arrival of a feeding parent. With a small slat on the blinds lifted askew, I have just enough visibility to observe, photograph, and enjoy the sight of the little yellow gaping mouths lifting upward for their parent-delivered meal. I make this climb onto the counter up to a dozen times daily. If I didn't have to crane my neck and lower back (due to the low ceiling) in order to make my observations, I would probably sit atop the counter for hours at a time watching those hungry little gold-rimmed mouths expanding out of proportion to the hatchlings' finger-sized, hairless, bloodmoon-red bodies. I've been invited to walk a beach at low tide with a friend this afternoon, something I love to do. I've also been invited to an afternoon movie as a celebratory break from several weeks of nonstop work. But only in the interest of nurturing important human relationships am I leaving the house for more than a couple of hours at a time. I know these hatchlings are growing into nestlings who will soon fledge; then I will never be sure which of the juncos in my yard are those I once spied as babies. I've got a precious slim window of ten to thirteen days during which I will be able to watch these several chicks grow bigger, develop feathers, and practice flapping their new wings.

It doesn't have to be about knowing everything related to biodiversity. We can go a long way toward protecting, by simply caring. By having a deep or meaningful experience with a particular species and fostering a sense of appreciation or even love. And we don't have to travel to seven continents to do so. We can do it in our back yards, local parks, a patch of dusty ground, a beach or pond, with a single rock …

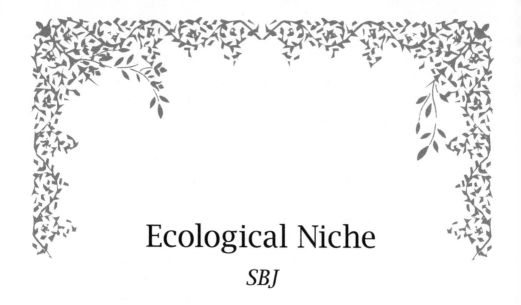

Ecological Niche

SBJ

We choose the niche that suits us best for life and living.

I began drafting this chapter in August 2017, early in my term as Fairmont State University (FSU) interim president, my fourth university presidency. Allow me to expand those drafted words to more thoughtfully develop the concept of ecological niche and apply it to my own metaphorical niche.

August 2017

In August 2017 at FSU, I welcomed some 100 football Falcons (70 percent returning; 30 percent first-time freshmen and transfers) to the fall semester. They arrived ten days before the start of classes, in time for two-a-days in preparation for the August 31 season opener when East Stroudsburg visited Duvall-Rosier Field in Fairmont, West Virginia. The athlete in me once more faced reality as I interacted with these fine young men.

In a photograph of me with the team, I'm the old weathered guy. I've witnessed a corollary scene many times when forestry fieldwork took me into second growth Appalachian hardwood forests, where abandoned hillside farms had yielded to succession. Picture a 19th century farmstead with tilled flatland, open pasture, and a rough apple orchard and garden near the home and outbuildings. Now imagine the buildings in decay, with oak, poplar, ash, maple, and hickory reclaiming the land (field, pasture, garden, and orchard), inexorably giving way to a maturing forest. The tilled land went quickly to poplar and ash. These full sunlight-demanding, wind-seeded species occupy the lowland, standing dense and reaching 80-100 feet. To the uninitiated, this stand seems ancient with large diameter individuals and open understory. The old pasture would have yielded to forest more slowly, having first transitioned to blackberry, grape vine, cedar, pine, hackberry, locust, and then oak, maple, hickory, and others. Stand structure suggests variable ages, heights, and stem densities.

The home site and outbuildings support a mixed forest, punctuated by a former cellar depression or two, and a remnant wall. Tree species and stand structure are far more varied than the tilled stand, yet no more complex than the former pasture. A walnut and several oaks, planted many years prior by the family, stand wide and sturdy, their crowns stretching and expanding before abandonment.

The former orchard presents yet another image, with the gnarled, ancient apple trees still surviving in the declining light beneath the developing forest of oaks, pine, sugar maple, and perhaps a walnut or two. The new stand rises vigorously above the venerable apple survivors. I see me (the apple tree) among the 18-22-year-old student athletes.

My days of youth and performance on the field have come and gone. The new growth represents the future. I am the historical artifact. Yet that is not all bad. The apple tree holds memory of the farm's glory days, and tells the tale for those able to read the powerful story of domestication, settlement, three human generations, abandonment, and reclamation. The apple tree provided habitat for the squirrel that planted the acorn, sheltered the young oak seedlings from scalding sun, and protected tender shoots from browsing deer. The youngsters survived and thrived in large measure because of the apple tree.

The young *trees* (football players) in the photo seemed that afternoon to appreciate the role we apple trees had played in their nurturing. They accept their role now as the successors, and honor the effort of those who pioneered and enabled.

I delivered a message to the team and coaching staff. I spoke only a few minutes, not long enough nor the right setting to delve into my lessons-from-nature theme. Instead, I related to them how my role as president mirrors football, how leading any enterprise embodies the same concepts and tenets. Simply, I said that as president, I coach (faculty, staff, administrators). As a coach, I evaluate and improve performance on our university field of play. In the process, I learn from my teammates, assess my own weaknesses, and compensate for them. I know that I must trust and depend upon others, each with their own unique strengths and skills. Like them and their coaches, I know the playbook and strive to call the right plays, assure proper execution, and inspire and motivate. In all university endeavors, I implore reaching beyond our grasp. I embrace rewarding excellence, celebrating success, and learning from failure. I insist of myself and other members of our team a focus on mission, working hard, staying fit (mentally, physically, emotionally, and spiritually), and having fun!

I did not describe myself as one of them. I admitted to being an old man (then 66 years), with a son two years senior to Tom Brady. Yet, I assured them that I begin each and every day with vigorous exercise. They exploded in applause and expressions of appreciation when I told them that just two days earlier I had bench-pressed 265 pounds. I mentioned that I am a former marathon runner (the full 26.2-mile distance). I reminded them that I remain addicted to living and to learning. That I am committed to serving. I quoted Helen Keller, who in her sunset years, observed that "Life is either a daring adventure, or nothing." I told them that my interim presidency is the latest chapter of my life's daring adventure. That their life as a Falcons football team player is certainly their own early-adult-life daring adventure.

The second growth forest can learn from the apple tree. Along life's journey, we all have opportunities to live, learn, serve, and lead. I honestly had not thought about the applicability of the remnant apple relict passing wisdom to his successional cohort until I viewed the photo of me with the vital football *trees* around me. Yet another set of lessons from nature. I had seen such apple tree survivors scores of times, indelibly tracing the measure and mark of man on the landscape a century or more into distant days of yore.

I like to think that throughout my time as FSU interim president, I had somehow enabled, inspired, and sculpted these future citizens.

Physical Niche

Now let's leave my afternoon with the Falcon football team behind. I just pulled my copy of *The Dictionary of Forestry* (1998 John A. Helms) from the shelf.

> Niche 1. The ultimate unit of the habitat, i.e. the specific spot occupied by an individual organism 2. By extension, the more or less specialized relationships existing between an organism or individual and its environment 3. The specific set of environmental and habitat conditions that permit the full development and completion of the life cycle of an organism...

The latter half of the definition (not excerpted) goes on to explain niche on a species basis. I will stick with the term as it applies to the individual. After all, I am an individual organism. I cannot represent all members of our species, nor can I draw conclusions from my own behavior and preferences applicable to others. Our species' niche now extends permanent habitation across six of the seven continents, from desert to rain forest and from Arctic to equatorial. That wide range suggests that we have demands and needs that are easily satisfied, non-specific, and nearly universal. More plausibly our range means that we are malleable, innovative, and able to make almost any place serve our needs for food, water, shelter, etc. We humans can tolerate, modify, adapt, and thrive across wide ranges.

My own personal preference spectrum, so far as I've tested, is far narrower. And most assuredly, I define my preferences beyond the basic animal niche measures of food, water, shelter, climate, and mates (we must assure continuing the species). These are both biological and physical metrics. My preferences include emotional and professional, which I'll develop more fully later.

Sure, a tropical clime might serve me well, excepting that my psyche demands four seasons. Even here in northern Alabama, our deciduous hardwoods stand leafless four-plus months. Our Big Blue Lake, where we reside, froze over convincingly twice during the 2017-18 winter. Neo-tropical songbirds pass through twice annually. Many waterfowl end their southern trek in our vicinity, including sandhill cranes and whooping cranes. We enjoyed a snow flurry or two and once an inch or so of accumulation. One unusual mid-winter storm of 2016-17 deposited nine inches!

Our home sits at 750 feet above sea level. Local relief separates the Tennessee River flood plain from the ridges just east of Huntsville by 1,000 feet. I like my land wrinkled. We once lived at 11 feet above sea level on Wilmington Island near Savannah, GA. We thought of it as a lovely spot and an enjoyable stopover for those brief years, yet we did not consider it a destination location. We bloomed there, ate lots of fresh shrimp, relished the summer morning sea-breeze front tropical rains, tremendous summer afternoon showers and storms, live oaks, Spanish moss, and explosive perennial and shrub gardens. Summer surrendered reluctantly to fall; fall gradually melded with spring; summer accepted the seasonal mantel in April. Long term, I need some semblance of winter, absent in coastal Georgia. The land stretched unwrinkled all the way inland to the fall line.

Fairbanks, Alaska certainly offered wrinkled land. The campus sat on a bluff at 800 feet above sea level. On moderately clear days we could see the central Alaska Range peaks at 12-14,000 feet. The clearest of days brought Denali (20,317 feet) into view far to the WSW. I shall forever cherish living in the near-Arctic for those four years, yet six months of way-deep winter kept us from long-season gardening, hiking, and enjoying the tranquil outdoors. Late spring and early summer brought man-eating platoons (squadrons) of mosquitoes and black flies. A permanent home demanding hats with mosquito-netting and Deep-Woods Off did not make for pleasant marital strolls and gardening! Again, we would not trade our four-year Alaska adventure for anything. Our present retrospective is, however: "Been there; done that!"

Wrinkled land, four seasons. Throw in annual rainfall adequate to support forests, preferably distributed across the year. Huntsville, Alabama averages 55 inches evenly distributed. Growing season rainfall is normally plentiful, often coming in entertaining thunderstorms. I need to add that as another criterion for my preferred niche. I don't yearn for tornado alley, yet I do like a dynamic summer atmosphere with rain and pyrotechnics!

We accessed our four-acre New Hampshire property from an unpaved road. Winter snow and ice covered, punctuated by periods of slush and mud, road conditions forced numerous periods when we could not enjoy our morning walks together, debriefing from the prior day and readying ourselves for what might lie ahead. We decided that we were not well-adapted country creatures, more suited instead for lighted neighborhoods with sidewalks. That's where we've landed. We are further removed from nature's wildness, yet we have critters adapted to sharing our neighborhood. I can find adequate levels of "wild" near at hand.

Shopping (groceries, odds and ends, and department stores) stood a distance from our N.H. home. Here in northern Alabama everything we need is within a few miles, as are farmland, nature trails, open space, greenways, and the Wheeler National Wildlife Refuge. Our daughter and two of our five grandkids live just six miles away. We can be at the Huntsville Airport, a nice regional service center, in 15 minutes. Interstate I-565 is seven miles south. Toss in our Big Blue Lake home location, and we have all that we need to compose our semi-retirement preferred niche.

Some would say we're too far from the ocean or that we don't have a major professional sports franchise, or ski slopes. Yet for Judy and me, this is our preferred physical niche. I suppose that Judy and I embraced each of our landings along the journey as *situational niches*. We viewed each location as a perfect waypoint. We did not so much declare any given location as simply a stopover, particularly once we left Alaska, which we knew would not extend to retirement. We did accept that the Ohio and New Hampshire presidencies could conceivably be endpoints. However, circumstances steered us otherwise. Each milepost offered satisfaction and reward. Every situational niche returned dividends in memories, experiences, and friends. Each move paved the way to the next. Every experience strengthened my leadership, wisdom, and knowledge tool kit. I learned at each situational niche how to better capitalize on the next.

Applicability of Maslow's Hierarchy

I imagined all along that we were simply living life and advancing career. I had not thought of the journey in more esoteric terms, until I devoted time, deep thought, and reflection to writing about the journey. I've learned that writing can be, perhaps should and must be, an act of creation and evolution. To this point, I had missed an obvious relevance of niche in human terms to Maslow's hierarchy of needs. So, I shall shift from what I as an individual *Homo sapiens* might minimally require to survive and reproduce, and write instead about seeking elements of Maslow's upper tier hierarchy. Maslow, a mid-twentieth century American psychologist, first published his theory on a human hierarchy of needs in a 1943 paper, "A Theory of Human Motivation," in *Psychological Review*. His *biological needs* constitute most of what I term the physical niche: food, water, shelter, safety, etc. *Belonging and love*, the next tier, derive from family, friends, spouse, and related. *Self-esteem* involves recognition, respect, and achievement of mastery in some aspect(s) of life, living, vocation, and avocation. His original theory crowned the hierarchy pyramid at *self-actualization*, constituting fulfillment, creativity, and realization of personal potential. I feel reasonably content that my career scratched that itch of attainment.

Maslow's thinking, however, evolved to recognize a yet higher-level need: *self-transcendence*. He wrote, "Transcendence refers to the very highest and most inclusive or holistic levels of human consciousness, behaving and relating, as ends rather than means, to oneself, to significant others, to human beings in general, to other species, to nature, and to the cosmos" (*Farther Reaches of Human Nature*, New York 1971, p. 269). He believed that we find such transcendence only when we serve a higher purpose, an outside goal, one involving altruism and spirituality.

I had not revisited Maslow in many years. How uncanny, I now find, that he would have considered my current life and post-career focus as transcendent. He actually speaks directly to seeking ends in service "to significant others, to human beings in general, to other species, to NATURE (my emphasis), and to the cosmos." That is my work, my aim, my life. Once more, I am humbled ... and, I feel inspired beyond measure.

That paragraph would serve as a statement of closure if I did not want to wrap other elements of niche into this chapter. I would have saved it for the end had it not been so necessary to offer it now. It provides Maslow's view and my own impetus for everything else about individual human niches. Such perspective also addresses fundamental truths for our species. I know that both Christianity and Islam speak to the transcendent obligation of humanity for such service "to significant others, to human beings in general, to other species, to nature, and to the cosmos." Without such transcendent aims, we cannot possibly sustain our species, steward our one Earth, and assure that we humans will be more than a brief footnote in the future fossil record. I believe that no other species embody intentional transcendent purpose.

From the esoteric and somewhat theological, I turn from Maslow and spirituality to elements of niche that have altered and directed my own life choices.

Emotional Niche

A great deal of what I have covered as physical niche involves emotional attraction, indifference, or revulsion. I recall completing my undergraduate forestry degree during a tough economic period (early '70s). Prospective employers were holding tight, delaying hires. I interviewed and accepted a very attractive position late in the semester, just a couple of weeks before graduation. I had cast a wide net of applications, with few location constraints. I wanted work in my field, and would have accepted relevant employment anywhere in the United States. That flexibility, along with excellent grades, three summers of employment in my field, consistent within-semester part time work, and a proven performance ethic, positioned me for securing work. I was one of the few to have an offer in hand.

My wife and I leaped at the chance to relocate to southeastern Virginia. We knew precious little about the locale, accepting the opportunity with glee. We believed we would serve there for the duration of our working lives, and we felt that we could thrive. In retrospect, we checked all but the wrinkled land criterion. We had each other, our families lived just seven hours away, and our two children arrived while we sank roots there. We considered our situation to be perfect. We had found our emotional (and physical) niche.

In fact, we learned how to adroitly create an acceptable emotional niche when the company (my employer) relocated us to Georgia and then to Alabama. The same proved true for our self-directed career moves in higher education that led us sequentially to New York, Pennsylvania, Alabama, North Carolina, Alaska, Ohio, New Hampshire, Alabama, West Virginia, and back to Alabama. I've said many times, "We decided to bloom wherever we were planted."

Professional Niche

We took control of the emotional factor, adopting and accommodating as necessary. Career determined the physical niche within broad limits. During my professional wanderings, we relied heavily upon fortuity and serendipity. After I had said that at some meeting, a colleague came to me saying, "I understand the role that serendipity played, but please explain *futility*." A lesson: always elucidate! Reminds me of a workshop that a Purdue University colleague and I presented on timber taxation to forest landowners in Pennsylvania. He correctly read confusion in his audience, paused, and said, "I guess I really fuzzed that up." Several of the end-of-day course evaluations conveyed this message, "I really liked Dr. Hoover's presentations, but I don't know why he felt need to use the 'F' word." He and I laughed heartily, yet took the same lesson to heart. Always elucidate! Never assume that what you say is heard or interpreted as intended. Nature normally keeps her lessons simple and clear. As should we. Nature seldom intends to be misunderstood.

I did not set out to be a university executive. It happened, and we capitalized on opportunities presented. I returned to university to obtain my Ph.D., not because I saw higher education positions as *the* desired end result, but because we wanted ingress to the kinds of positions a doctoral degree could open. Once I became *Dr.* Jones, we chose from among five different positions and divergent pathways, each presented with some level of assurance that it could be mine: a forest resources faculty position at Penn State University, U.S. Forest Service research project leader, purchasing and heading an existing consulting forestry firm, an executive position within a forest products industry trade association, and an international post within the company I had served for 12 years. We chose Penn State, way led to way, and that decision has made all the difference. We had developed a matrix of pros and cons, giving the impression that we applied a definitive formula for an iron-clad decision. Yet our decision wavered, ebbed, and flowed. We made our choice, and decided to not second guess ourselves. We chose our professional niche, and made the most of it. Fortuity and serendipity reign supreme.

Nature does as well. The acorn does not decide where the squirrel caches it. Instead, evolution and genotype equip the seed to make the most of wherever the acorn germinates and sprouts. If in shallow soil on an upper convex, southwest facing slope, forget about aspirations to be The Mighty Oak. Instead, if cached in leaf litter at the deep-soil base of a concave northeast facing lower slope, the same acorn can reign supreme. Fortuity and serendipity!

Judy and I, to the best of our ability, evaluated the five sites, selecting what we felt were the conditions and place best suited to us, and our aspirations. We could have done far worse. We are both abundantly blessed by the aggregate result of deliberate choices, conscious adoption of positive attitude, and a willingness to explore and exploit. We have achieved self-actualization. I am now reaching upward for self-transcendence. I never grow tired of quoting Louis Bromfield, mid-twentieth century author (30 bestsellers) and playwright. He bought what he described as "an old, worn-out Ohio farm" in 1939, and dedicated his life to rehabilitating it. He wrote of his passion in his non-fiction book *Pleasant Valley*:

"The adventure at Malabar is by no means finished ... The land came to us out of eternity and when the youngest of us associated with it dies, it will still be here. The best we can hope to do is to leave the mark of our fleeting existence upon it, to die knowing that we have changed a small corner of this Earth for the better by wisdom, knowledge, and hard work."

Changing a small corner of this Earth for the better is my self-transcendent mission and quest. Such is the professional and personal life niche I now occupy.

Temporal Niche

I've come to accept that nothing is permanent; stasis does not exist in nature. Niche, therefore, has a temporal component. The parameters defining a given place shift with time; our own preferred niche features change as we navigate life's journey.

Even during those stages of my life and career when things seemed to be at stasis, they were not. We spent nine years at Penn State. A lot transpired during that period. Matt went from fifth grade to a rising college junior. Katy more than doubled her age. We lost both my dad and Judy's. The Blizzard of '93 left its permanent positive mark on my psyche. During those nine years of then-perceived stasis, the sun rose and set 3,285 times. Spring wildflowers filled central Pennsylvania's forests nine times, and each spring I regretted not venturing out into those vernal woods enough. As we left State College, PA, I wished I had done better at saying goodbye to my dad (and Judy's). I'm slowly learning that regrets come at the cost of opportunities foregone. I can only pledge to take better advantage of every moment presented. I am likewise committed now to flush (and in doing so, refresh) lessons from long-dormant memories of days and experiences long-past.

Everything is static without the passage of time. For that reason, stasis does not exist in nature! Nor does it in life and living. Perhaps only does the wisdom of age awaken us to the movement of time, the pace of life, and the precious dimensions of each moment. I want to slow time, cling to special moments. Capture life through mind, body, heart, soul, and spirit. I've lived more than 24,000 days. My future upon graduating from high school stretched on nearly forever. Each day meant so much less then. Now, the hourglass holds most of the sand grains at the lower level, yet they continue to cascade through that far too wide funnel at a pace that seems to increase with age. Only now do I see the truth my maternal grandmother dispensed about time accelerating with age.

I wonder what to make of this stage of life, this temporal niche. I will call it my awakening. The alarm is sounding the call to opening the portals to absorb every moment through all senses. To first believe, and then to look, see, feel, and act. To absorb, sort, and comprehend the truth. To interpret and translate nature's lessons for those who share this journey, and for those who will follow. I have reached the point when I want to leave bread crumbs so that others may find their way.

Niche: Drawing Lessons for Life and Living

My August interaction with the football guys served as witness that every circumstance, business opportunity, family situation, workplace crisis, and personal episode can be viewed in the context of an organism within its environment, as a cog within an ecosystem complex. This approach permits me to apply lessons from nature. That's how I entered my Fairmont State University interim presidency. Entering a new specific environment, I asked myself how I could bring my skills, experience, and wisdom to lift an institution at no small level of risk.

I spoke often to diverse audiences and FSU stakeholders of my *calling* to the six-month assignment, characterizing my task in terms that spoke to a *cause* that is spiritual, sacred, and noble, effecting change that will be transcendent. My message communicated as much, even though I may not have employed the actual word *transcendent*. It is only now as I reflect that I saw the interim presidency as seeking "the very highest and most inclusive or holistic levels of human consciousness, behaving and relating, as ends rather than means." I was not advancing my career; this was a career postscript. I perceived my leadership goal as transcendent, making an institution far better than it had come to expect.

I characterized the university's location as a fertile lower concave slope, rich with possibilities, yet suffering declining revenue and enrollment, and satisfied with performance one might expect with a more impoverished upper convex anchorage. Too often, in life and enterprise, we give short shrift to our own potential, limiting our reach to what we can now grasp, failing to extend beyond what is adequate and comfortable. The oak seedling doesn't require a conscious site assessment nor does it self-assess. It simply does what it does. Reach vertically and outward for light, and send roots to tap available soil moisture and nutrition. The site imposes limits. The tree's genotype commands its roots and leaves to gather what resources are available. There is no second guessing and self-doubt, no lack of confidence, in nature. No fear of failure. No reluctance to act.

Evolution locks presumptive success into an individual's DNA, along with innate judgment of risk and consequence. Squirrels seem to *know* what branches are within leaping reach. Those who leap beyond what is safe are less likely to extend that risky behavior trait forward. The same consequence befalls the dove who waits milliseconds too long in reacting to the hawk's shadow. The night mouse who pays too little heed to the owl's soft wingbeat. The concept of niche implies that individuals and species perform most effectively when they reside where their senses are best attuned. Where their skills, wisdom, and knowledge serve them well. The same seems to be true of business, enterprise, and life. We decide where and how, and do what works best for us as individuals.

This may be a stretch to suggest an allegory, but I changed my major at one point to paper science engineering, what I've since characterized as a kind of applied organic chemistry. I learned quickly with my first semester of different subjects that for me organic chemistry served as a substrate within which I could not find purchase, sink roots, or understand palpably as something real. I am grateful to have discovered early that my niche lay in forestry and applied ecology. I have never regretted choosing a field suitable for my inner wiring, passion, purpose, and grasp. I suppose that there are other disciplinary niches I might have exploited, yet I cannot imagine a tack that would have suited me better.

I cannot imagine greater self-actualization and certainly no better suited vehicle for self-transcendence! I am at home; I am at peace. I am doing what I do best. In service to the future, *to nature, and to the cosmos.*

I ponder whether any other organism in nature seeks transcendence. The soaring eagle may from our perspective seem transcendent, yet I suspect that she is simply hunting the way that suits her best. I picture the mountain goat grazing high above the Denali valley tundra and think such an existence is a form of transcendence. More objectively, I believe the goat, in his own sure-footed way, is simply gaining sustenance and avoiding wolves and grizzly predation. Likewise, I believe that the king salmon, by leaping rapids and falls, is simply assuring the next generation's success. I see no reach for transcendence behind the life cycle of hatching, surviving the trip downriver as fry, and then growing to saltwater adulthood, before following clues at maturity back to the source waters to repeat the parents' cycle, again and again and again, forevermore.

We choose the niche that suits us best for life and living. I take comfort that I have found the "specific set of environmental and habitat conditions that permit the full development and completion" of my own life cycle. We have embraced situational niches along our life and career journey. We advanced toward self-actualization with each career and life twist and turn. We are now where we choose to be as we reach for self-transcendence. Each pathway selection shaped our journey and our life. Again, way has led on to way. That has made all the difference. No longer a situational niche, this is our destination niche.

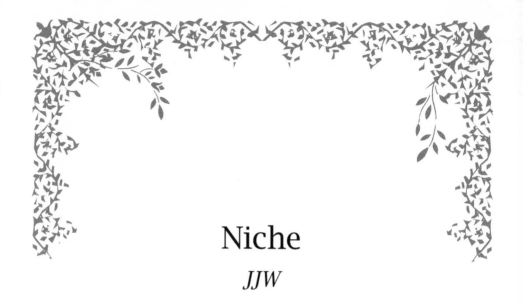

Niche

JJW

An **ecological niche** is the role and position a species has in its environment; how it meets its needs for food and shelter, how it survives, and how it reproduces. A species' niche includes all of its interactions with the biotic and abiotic factors of its environment.

One of my favorite poets, Mary Oliver, crafted a sublime phrase at the end of her famous "Wild Geese." Interjected among lines about penitence, despair, and loneliness are references back to the beauty and ongoing presence of nature, and its ability to repeatedly give itself to us.

The last line tells us that the natural world beckons: "announcing your place in the family of things." And as I briskly walked the hilly unpaved roads early this morning—meditating on the notion of ecological niche as a metaphor for human living—I heard myself reciting this poem. I had already seen the frequently visiting hummingbird, swallows dancing in dawn arcs, soft pink clouds swiftly blowing overhead, and fir trees in gentle motion: all before leaving our cottage. My walk was punctuated by a female black-tailed deer and her spotty fawn skirting the edge of a neighbor's field to browse the blackberry bushes; the sunlight rubbing a madrona trunk into fiery auburn splendor; and two bald eagles in tandem flight. An unexpected gift, Oliver's words came rushing in, verses I had memorized years ago but which were now suddenly imbued with deeper meaning: niche, ecological niche. It suddenly became clear to me that the final phrase of this iconic ode to nature as healer is exactly how I view "niche" as metaphor. Our niche is our place in the interconnected web of all life.

From the definition of ecological niche, I extract three vital ideas: survival, role, and relationships. This is what an ecological niche is; it is the way in which a species carries out its living in relationship to others and its environment. The biotic and abiotic features of the location are important. But even more foundational to this message of niche is the "how and effect" of a particular species. How lions respond to prey and predators, what their effect is on the other living creatures, how they impact and are impacted by the plants and landscape features in which they reside. Ecological niche refers to the process a species engages as it strives to stay alive and safe, as it performs its role in the community of life, as it encounters and interacts with others.

We cannot forget that we are individual members *of a species*: *Homo sapiens*. What happens to any single human, also happens to our species as a whole. It is impossible, and very impractical, to separate one human from the species "human." This chapter proceeds with a brief look at how viewing survival, role, and relationships in our own lives— particularly as these are manifested in our body, emotions, mind, and spirit—can lead us to greater awareness of our effect, as *one of many* of our species, on this web of life of which we are all, inextricably, a part.

Survival

Crucially, we need to survive bodily. For without our physical presence, we cannot sense, feel, think, pray, or otherwise engage in this journey of being a human on Earth. With nonhuman animals, there is such a strong demarcation between breath and death. For example, we rarely see the wild coyote transitioning, ailing in a mortal and ultimate surrender to breathlessness; most often we see either the vibrant, hunting, running pup, or the finished coyote lying inert on the side of a road. But we humans are much more alert to ourselves and to one another, noticing the progression of illness and disability in our aging elders, or marking the birthdays and milestones of our children; these transitions we make it our business to note. That our concept of "survival" is a complex construct stands in sharp contrast to the ease with which our daily needs can be met. The amenities, technology, devices, and privileges of modern everyday life in developed countries in the 21st century easily render access to resources, medical interventions, or food; at the touch of a button or a short drive away we can receive life-sustaining care or sustenance. It's so easy, in fact, that many of us take it for granted. This is not to shame those with plenty, or to denounce the structures that situate such basic amenities at the back of our minds. It is simply to call to mind that survival for *all* humans is not that facile.

The bodily-sustaining, safe-keeping needs of food, clean water, shelter, and health are to be honored and remembered. For though we consider them basic rights, we are seeing a global surge of deaths and violence over water rights, food scarcity, and housing in an overpopulated world with numerous vast areas of poor infrastructure and technology, climate change induced hardships, and ideological strife. How we survive (or don't) and who has access to limited resources (at the expense of whom) are key aspects of defining our niche. By simply opening up our awareness to the entire human system to which we belong—as well as the larger family of all life on the planet—we can begin to see how bodily survival is more than a concept; it is the very moment-by-moment struggle of members of our own species.

Our bodies are not the only way we survive in the world; emotional viability is also fundamental to our experience as humans. We have been blessed with such a vast array of fluid emotions. They come and go, fleeting as an unseen breeze. We have come to regard some emotions as especially desirable (particularly those that feel good to us), and others as emotions to deny, eradicate, "fix," or otherwise move through. These rich inner stirrings are all—each and every one of them—deeply valuable to us. I have a mentor who likes to remind me that emotional discomfort is "good information"; it alerts me to the need to pay attention. This is not unlike a hunger pang or a sore throat; the former indicates a need to eat (in order to sustain ourselves!) while the latter might tell us we are getting a cold, are overtired, or otherwise need to tend to our physical health. Emotions do this too. If I am uncomfortable with the way the harsh stranger treated me yesterday when I rang his doorbell at precisely the moment of our prearranged appointment, then that discomfort is telling me something: that perhaps I should abandon the meeting with this unsafe and unsavory character. This type of awareness keeps me safe, emotionally; it helps me *survive*.

I am of the group of people who believe that denying the emotions we don't prefer is actually harmful to us. At the very least we miss out on the opportunity to live a full and whole life as a human. There are tacit yet very real gifts in even the most difficult emotions. When I was grieving the death of a beloved friend, for example, I was able to also find gratitude for and hope in the legacy that my dear one left behind. Her writing, professional work, the people she had mentored, and her family continue to carry on her voice and wisdom long after her passing. As members of families, communities, workplaces, organizations, regions—and as humans who reside in geographies and landscapes with nonhuman species—our emotions can detrimentally or beneficially impact those around us. Acting on unprocessed emotions such as hatred, fear, and anger can harm those with whom we interact; behaving out of compassion and peacefulness positively grows our interdependence with people, places, flora, fauna. Our emotional health and capacity are directly linked to our survival via the impact they have on others.

Turning now to our mind, our human capacity for cognitive functioning: what does survival at a cognitive level look like? At its most basic, we understand how to: consume healthy foods, choose a safe community in which to live, stay out of the way of speeding cars (or, in our human beginnings, wild predators). We get that there are rudimentary pieces of knowledge that are key to our survival. Beyond that, surviving intellectually might entail exposing ourselves to the kind of stimuli that keep us on the path of learning. My graduate education took place at an institution that prided itself on "lifelong learning" and self-directed learning. In part, this means choosing and being motivated to seek out knowledge, including that which strengthens one's ability to survive in social and professional settings, as a global citizen, and personally, in a way that sustains the learner.

But as humans with the ability to think critically, we can also use our good brains to broaden our concept of niche (our environment) to include the entire planet—cultures, religious practices, customs, values of humans we do not encounter in our everyday life but who are, nonetheless, part of our human family. For example, we are increasingly unable to deny the finger-touch global community in which we reside, no matter whether we use the Internet or not. Trade, politics, religion, economy, travel, climate change all occur on a grand scale and in places to which we have never traveled; yet we are one body: the human species. We have the capacity, too, to remember our nonhuman kin— creatures and plants that we have never seen, geographies we have not yet experienced, Earth forces and weather, geology and interstellar interactions—all those entities that share this planet and this galaxy. We employ our intellect to understand the intricate ways in which we need one another, the whole beautiful undeniably exquisite weaving without which we could not exist.

Next, we can use the notion of spirituality to offer insight into how we survive as a species. I use the term "spirituality" very distinctly from "religion." The latter is sectarian and rooted in common beliefs *within* a particular sect. I view spirituality more broadly: many people of various traditions can be spiritual in that they seek connection with something greater than us (a power higher than humans). There is huge significance in deeply rooted religious conviction. And I believe that there are myriad paths to connection with the divine.

I think of one's spiritual niche as the way in which we pursue faith in something larger than ourselves. We are given, in the human condition, birth and death. It is the life we lead between those beginning and end markers that characterizes something about our ecological niche and spirit. Faith is part of how we thrive on this journey. For those reading this who do not claim a particular sect as their structure for a spiritual life, there are activities like creating something new—art, poetry, music— that also afford us a connection with a source, a powerful presence of something we cannot see or name, but which may very well inspire the creative works we do. Having something in which to believe, be in awe, and be inspired takes our species to a more profound level of existence.

Survival of individuals—bodily, emotionally, mentally, spiritually— connects us to survival as a species. Our understanding of how to maintain ourselves begins at the individual level and moves to larger and larger scales: one human, a family, the community, nation, continent, the entire globe of humanity. When we learn to behave as one person *within the context* of this ultimately global and shared existence as "the human species," we realize our ability to survive: "survival" in its most profound definition.

Practical Survival for Our Species

1. Body: Consider your own access to clean water, food, shelter, and healthcare. Locate a community of people whose access to these life-sustaining elements is compromised or nonexistent. Make a commitment to reach out and support that community in some way (monetary donation, in-kind gift, service work, crowdfunding, outreach, publicity, etc.).
2. Emotion: Consider what unmet emotional needs you have and begin to pay attention to meeting those needs. (Are you unduly stressed out? Have unresolved resentments at a friend or family member? Need support working through an issue? Feel uncomfortable with something?) Commit to doing something monthly to support the emotional needs of someone you know. (Make them dinner. Send a greeting card. Listen to them.)
3. Mind: Consider how you might increase your knowledge about another culture or religion. Commit to finding someone from that region, race, or geography from whom you can learn.
4. Spirituality: Consider the things in your life that are sources of awe, inspiration, creativity, or spiritual guidance. Make a commitment to accessing that source on a daily basis, and finding others with whom you can share your experiences.

Role

The role we enact is very much a bodily engagement, and very much impacts those around us. When those of us who are working folks consider our paid employment, we can see that our niche must include the tangible tools we need to perform that work. These might include implements (the carpenter's hammer, the writer's pen, the office worker's computer). But our bodies—our physicality—in our work also demand that we do work of which we are capable. As a middle-aged woman, I no longer have the stamina to spend all day teaching children with special needs; that work of my early first career demanded heavy lifting, manipulation of children's physical support equipment (i.e., wheelchairs), and exceedingly long days of teaching preceded by preparation, and followed by data collection, analysis, and reporting. I loved that work of my youth. But as my body wearied and my passions shifted, I found decreasing satisfaction or capacity to do it.

When we imagine the other kinds of roles we have in the world—maintaining a home and yard, tangibly giving to those in our closest circle, our position in the local community—recognizing our shifting physical limits and potential (even as we age and ail) are vital to being vibrant members of society. And, remembering to expand our awareness to the global community affords us a chance to make a larger contribution to the collective work of humanity. We can further search out how the movements of our bodies as we engage our work and play impact the natural environment ("biotic and abiotic factors"). Our gas-consuming vehicles, travel in jet planes (noise and air polluting), consumption of exotic (or endangered) flora and fauna via foods, medicines, clothing, cosmetics, and household goods are one aspect we can explore. We also have the labor of beautiful fellow humans whose work in places far from ours might be considered an inexpensive amenity; remembering where our goods are made, by whom, under what conditions can refocus us on the role our bodies (and others') play in the complex functioning of this vast planet.

Our emotional lives impact the role we have in the world too. In our occupation, we can deepen our understanding of our niche by noticing how satisfied (or not) we are in how we spend the workweek. Most of us have had the experience of working with others who have long since stopped feeling good about the work they are doing; perhaps we have been that person in the workplace at one time or another. Our emotional landscape in our jobs impacts others in countless ways: the grump, the cheerleader, the quietly productive person. As we reexamine our perspective on how we feel in the work we do, our emotional niche or role becomes clearer. Our emotional *modus operandi* might be really helpful to those around us, particularly if we tend to be the cheery or very cooperative one—boosting others' morale and taking on additional tasks that are not assigned to us. Seeing our emotional niche—how it impacts others as well as *how we feel* about how we feel—gives us the opportunity to make small shifts that might be necessary for long-term wellbeing. Giving too much (so that we feel overly spent, or resentful, at the end of the day) is one indicator that we are not well-sustaining ourselves in our emotional niche.

Intellectually we play a role too. The simplest way of looking at cognition in the work or position we hold is to consider what we do and don't know in order to perform that role. Sometimes this is about having enough education or training specific to the work or position we carry out. But—blurring lines between body, emotion, and mind—humans can also look at the intersecting factors that entail a sense of wellbeing as we work. Are the tasks or issues we are to meet and solve from day to day within easy reach; that is, do they overly tax us, under-stimulate us, or do we feel pretty good?

Spirituality cannot be omitted from a discussion about our roles as members of concentrically larger spheres of influence. Some ways that spirit manifests in an individual's role in community include calling, purpose, and inspiration. We do our work, our job, our tasks. And how much do we feel part of something larger? How much do we carry the sense of purpose that whatever we do is just one part of a greater being and doing? How inspired are we to continue with all the mundane activities of the moment with the conviction that the outcome is more far-reaching than the actual small task? One way I know to connect with that larger sense of purpose is via volunteer work. Since I was a candy striper at the age of twelve, I have carried a continual commitment, in one form or another, to service work in the communities in which I have lived, as well as in short stints in regions far from my home place. This is one way we can offer ourselves, take on a role, that allows us to feel inspired, to offer inspiration, and to reap the gifts of having given of ourselves "just because we can." Volunteerism is a free offering; we are not being remunerated. Somehow my passion for community service always falls into the category of spiritual offering, I think simply because it is not required. (Though I believe the world would be a much more peaceful, bright place if every human on the planet offered himself freely, in addition to whatever expected or paid roles we already carry in our communities.)

These ruminations about survival, role, and relationships are much more complex than the scope of a short chapter can necessarily offer. Yet, they give us a starting point for assessment, re-examination, and the potential to make adjustments (significant or tiny) that will shift us back to a more balanced position in our environment, in the world of all living beings … which leads us directly into a mention of relations with others.

Practical Roles for Our Species

1. Body: Consider your capacity for your profession or vocation. Make a commitment to shift away from physically-depleting and materially-consumptive ways of engaging your work and responsibilities.
2. Emotion: Consider how your emotional landscape (habitual reactions to others and events) impacts the people around you at work or at home on a daily basis. Commit to civility (respectful politeness of heart and action) by taking time every day for quiet contemplation and restoring right relations with others when you have behaved disrespectfully or unkindly.
3. Mind: Consider your mental wellbeing and knowledge as they relate to your daily activities. Commit to refining your tasks and increasing your learning in order to efficiently meet your responsibilities.
4. Spirit: Consider what role you play in your community that is separate from your paid work or everyday responsibilities. Make a commitment to serve (or increase your service to) your community as a volunteer.

Relationships

Our ecological niche is largely focused on *how we are* with others. We can start by looking at our friendships and relations with our family.

I happen to live in a culture in which huge geographic separations exist between family and friends. Email, telephones, Skype, and the postal service carry the messages of which my relationships are comprised. In recent years, it has even gotten stranger for me: I call "dear" some people with whom these at-a-distance communications have been the sole definition of our relationship; that is, I have not met in person some of the people with whom I have developed friendships, collegial or professional ties, with whom I work, or collaborate. My physical residence and place on the planet are not proximate to many with whom I interact on a daily basis. But my body is absolutely and irrevocably intertwined with the natural world that is my physical environment. I have chosen to call "home" a geography that is not my birth place, or anything like my hometown. I grew up in a sunny, hot, paved over, highly populated, noisy urban setting; I have chosen (or been chosen by?) a landscape that is rural, wet, quiet, heavily-treed, and abounding with wild flora and fauna. I merely walk out my front door and place my hands on the bare Earth in order to stay in deep, active, engaged relationship with my natural environment. Thinking about whom and with what we choose to have in-person, tangible, interactive relationships in this world, and the means by which we do so, can shed light on this aspect of niche and interconnection.

But we can also consider how we respect or have reciprocity with others in relationship, an emotional aspect of "connection with." Though I hesitate to give only brief mention to a hugely significant issue that is front and center of the local and international daily news, it is difficult not to include in this overview of niche as metaphor respect for those with whom we feel emotionally distant. Difference can do this: race, sexual orientation, all the 'isms' we see plastering the newspaper, language, religion, politics. But the stark reality is that we all inhabit this one Earth and our predominant focus on distinctness over sameness keeps us emotionally at bay from our human kin. (And this is just the beginning point; looking at nonhuman creatures as kin is the next leap after this.) Our emotional relationship to what we perceive as "other" is largely reliant upon our primal need for safety in the forests and deserts of our human beginning: "other" often equaled "danger" in small tribal communities in which relationships with the known (ecological as well as human) were bound by intimacy, geography, and mutual survival. A stranger (human or beast) signaled an alert: invader, enemy, threat to survival and resources. But the transition away from this has been a slow one; we have vast territories governed, structured, and held in place so that a single newcomer is not a danger. Today we have myriad means for understanding, finding community with, "the different other" and this primal reflex of fear or apprehension *could* so easily be relic of our early human evolution. But this requires a commitment on our part: to decide that broader and more diverse communities, peace and understanding, embrace of difference actually create more safety and wellbeing for all of us than do divisions and sectarianism.

Cognitively, mentally, intellectually, we can learn from and teach one another—piecing back together the fabric of humanity as well as the natural environments on Earth—toward a community that is dynamic, fluid, fully alive and in vibrant relationship with all its parts. For humans are just one part of the whole environment of towns, nations, the planet, galaxies, and the universe. We can understand difference and sameness. The emotional reflex of "the fear of" can be tempered by the education and relationship building of one with another. Consider the simple example of cultural exchange: families hosting a foreign student in their home; sharing their meals, culture, and traditions with one another; building relationships of respect, love, and tolerance. This is us: we *are* the human family. We *are* the ecological community.

And if we can make a small emotional embrace, the simple willingness to learn from, and then find the spiritual largesse to reach beyond our own faith borders, we will truly have our real and perceived needs and desires met in acknowledgment of our shared residence on this Earth. We can find that spiritual generosity via compassion for ourselves and others, gratitude practices, and a faith community that opens us in acceptance, embracing and welcoming others—and "the perceived other."

Practical Relationships for Our Species

1. Body: Consider the various relationships in your life and how you are situated in relation to those others (geography, type

of relationship, means of communication, etc.). Commit to deepening those relationships that support you in being your best self.

2. Emotions: Consider all the relationships (intimate, acquaintances, strangers) in your life. Make a commitment to developing new relationships with people who feel a bit different from you.

3. Mind: Consider the way in which you limit relationships (i.e., the type of activities you do with a particular person, the attributes you consider for friendship, etc.). Commit to expanding the way in which you relate to others, including with nonhuman others.

4. Spirit: Consider how you practice gratitude and compassion on a sustained basis. Make a commitment to random acts of kindness (daily? weekly? monthly?), and express gratitude each and every day as soon as you wake up.

Mary Oliver's poem didn't specify the divisions that *we* use as demarcations to wall us off. It did not say what that "family" should look like or where they live. It did not regard creed, affiliation, colors, or qualities. The wise poet calls us to be one with all humans (who are all of equal value) and all nonhuman beings (who are all of equal value). She makes it clear and simple and equivalent by the use of her word "things": our place "in the family of things." This is our niche: our role, position, the way in which we meet needs, survive, reproduce in the environment of this planet, Earth. In dynamic interaction with all the living and physical parts of this sumptuous round blue-green environment we jointly share and inhabit, this niche is our place in kinship with all.

The Spirit of Nature

SBJ

"I come into the presence of still water. And I feel above
me the day-blind stars waiting with their light. For a
time, I rest in the grace of the world, and am free."
Wendell Berry, *New Collected Poems*

"It's the great, big, broad land 'way up yonder,
It's the forests where silence has lease;
It's the beauty that fills me with wonder,
It's the stillness that fills me with peace."
Robert Service, *Spell of the Yukon*

"The whole world of nature is a theater
representative of the glory of the Lord."
Emanuel Swedenborg, *Arcana Coelestia 3000*

I am a lifelong nature devotee, enthusiast, and student (B.S. Forestry;
Ph.D. Applied Ecology). Each decade has brought me closer to fully
embracing that my relationship to nature is deeply spiritual, a sacred
connection, as both Robert Service and Emanuel Swedenborg so
clearly implied and artfully articulated. I accept and embrace my
Earth stewardship obligation as similarly of a higher, core order. I began
contemplating this spiritual dimension more seriously and deliberately

as the president of Urbana University (Ohio), established originally as a Swedenborgian University. Via that presidency, I came to know the teachings of Emanuel Swedenborg, who recognized and voiced the absolute correspondence between spirit and man.

Semi-retired, I post a weekly essay devoted to nature-inspired life and living. I often weave the sacred and spiritual dimension into my posts, and the theme extends through both of my prior books.

My March 20, 2018 post offered reflections on my first-time intimate tour of nearby Cane Creek Canyon Nature Preserve, and spoke to the spiritual and sacred relationship the owners have with the land:

> Once Faye had left us, I rode in the back of the ATV, snapping an occasional photo between jostles and bounces. One photo revealed what I did not see. I simply intended to capture the nice bench placed at a ledge overhang along the trail. Instead, the sun's rays gave the scene an aura (the rays streaming from the ledge above giving the image a haloed essence), leading me to dub this The Altar. The entire preserve expressed an ethereal character. I felt the spiritual in multiple places that day. Too, I sensed in Jim and Faye a connection to the land of a sacred nature. They do obviously love the land and draw as much *from* it as they give *to* it. I'm reminded of Aldo Leopold's remark about caring for the land, "We can only be ethical in relation to something we can see, understand, feel, love, or otherwise have faith in." I feel certain that Jim and Faye are guided by understanding and love for the preserve, which is itself in whole an altar of sorts.

And continuing my post:

> As I reflect on our wonderful visit to Cane Creek Canyon, I recall an apt Wendell Berry quote: "Outdoors we are confronted everywhere with wonders; we see that the miraculous is not extraordinary, but the

common mode of existence. It is our daily bread." The miraculous features at Cane Creek Canyon are indeed not extraordinary, but are the common mode. Nature, in its many variants, is my daily bread. I am certain the same is true for Jim and Faye. I am grateful that nature enthusiasts like the Lacefields have taken giant steps to make this small corner of the world better through wisdom, knowledge, and hard work. They are Earth stewardship warriors.

Again, I am both humbled and inspired by the preserve and its intrepid magicians who have dedicated their lives to its care and conservation.

My Spiritual Journey and Intimacy with Nature

Late in 2015, I applied (unsuccessfully, I might add) for the presidency of a faith-based university. The process required a one-page Personal Faith Journey. I offer that statement here, exactly as I submitted it in November 2015:

"My parents were committed Methodists (steady, not devout) who molded us kids in a Christian home, with two loving parents, exemplifying adherence to the rocks of Faith, character, integrity, and strong values. I've never drifted from full embrace of moral and ethical character. I do admit, however, to straying through a period of agnosticism in my early professional years. My Faith has gradually grown over the years, perhaps too slowly up until age 50 or so. I progressed from a scientist who believed that nature and the study of it, in itself, provided all the answers I needed. I grew to a maturity that saw in nature a power, glory, and magnificence that could only be designed by an Eminence. Today, I am firmly convinced that my life has been guided by the

Hand of God, and that I have a deep obligation to do good in this world. Allow me several short reflections to illustrate seminal benchmarks in my personal Faith journey:

- The Urbana University Board hired me (2008) as President of that Swedenborgian-rooted institution, founded in 1850 by The Church of The New Jerusalem. During my tenure, the Board, with two-thirds secular members, pushed via that majority to distance UU even further from its sectarian roots. I held firm. I had said well before then that I recognize four levels of individual fitness, each necessary for a meaningful life well-lived: mental; physical; emotional; spiritual. I did not want to see UU drift even deeper into secular fog.

- May 3, 2012 – a rogue motorist (suspended license, illegally tagged large SUV) ran a neighborhood stop sign in broad daylight, plowing into Judy and me as we walked, hurtling us through the air. He left the scene; we found ourselves in separate ambulances rushing to the hospital. A neighbor who witnessed the impact and our ejection forward said later, "You were both caught by angels." We believe it… and we thank God for giving us a second chance. We are mostly recovered, living a subsequent, more purpose-driven life, and are grateful for each minute.

- March 2014 – our daughter's second child arrived six weeks early, at low weight. The hospital released Katy and little Sam after only two days. The first night at home (in Madison, AL; Judy and I were there by then), tiny Sam spent a restless, frightening (for us) night. By morning his temperature had dropped into the low 90s. Judy, Katy, and son-in-law Mike rushed Sam to the hospital. I stayed with six-year-old Jack. During the morning, Judy called as Jack and I hiked a forested trail. She reported that a team of doctors and nurses was working hard on Sam, and that she was afraid. Jack and I walked and talked; I prayed and fought tears, occasionally sobbing. I pledged to God that if

He would save Sam, I would devote my life to His service. Blessedly, Sam is now twenty months old and all is well!

My Faith journey continues, by no measure complete. Regardless, I am ready, willing, eager, and able to lead and inspire a sectarian university like yours."

I thought about modifying the statement for the purpose of this chapter to emphasize the role that nature has played in guiding my faith journey. Upon rereading it, I thought better, deciding to leave it untouched. As for the three sub-paragraphs, each is already rooted deeply in my view of nature as spiritual. Swedenborg's teachings brought me to a profound awakening of the intimate interplay among nature, man, and spirit. The SUV plowing into us cemented my acceptance that life is fleeting and fragile, and that there are no guarantees for tomorrow, steering me toward greater purpose. As for the third, it's so fitting and powerful that young Jack and I were hiking on the Rainbow Mountain Trail when Sam's outlook seemed most dim. As I edit these words, Sam is just a week shy of his fifth birthday, a gift and a blessing beyond measure. I often think of that spring day, walking the trail in despair and fervent prayer. I am always nearer to what I feel is a higher power, purpose, and cause when surrounded by nature's beauty, magic, wonder, and awe. I shall continue to devote my life to a greater calling, to changing some small corner of this Earth for the better through wisdom, knowledge, and hard work.

Aldo Leopold, a founding patriarch of American conservation and naturalist-philosopher, spoke of nature and spirit both explicitly and by implication. His land ethic constituted a spiritual relationship of man to the Earth. He wrote lyrically, powerfully, and poetically with compelling prose. His account of "a fierce green fire dying" in the eyes of a mother wolf he and his colleagues had shot speaks of a sacred connection between man and a magnificent beast. A spiritual fire kindled within him at that moment and carried through the remainder of his life, deepening the purpose and passion that fueled him.

"We reached the old wolf in time to watch a fierce green fire dying in her eyes. I realized then, and have known ever since, that there was something new to me in those eyes—something known only to her and to the mountain. I was young then, and full of trigger-itch; I thought that because fewer wolves meant more deer, that no wolves would mean hunters' paradise. But after seeing the green fire die, I sensed that neither the wolf nor the mountain agreed with such a view."

Aldo Leopold, A *Sand County Almanac and Sketches Here and There*

Leopold carried that haunting image with him the rest of his life, symbolizing that every cog in the wheel has value and purpose, and that all things are interconnected and interdependent. He seemed to suggest that the wolf is the imponderable numenon (Leopold's term for the intangible essence) of the ecosystem.

I view the wolf encounter as a critical juncture in Leopold's personal faith journey. Life changes us, whether SUV-induced, or the emotional collision as a fierce green fire dimmed in a wolf's eyes. Spiritual is a state of mind, a conscious awakening, and an embrace of higher purpose, meaning, and power. Each day deepens my appreciation for nature and furthers my own belief that I have work yet to do to honor a pledge I made along a trail on a March day of terrifying prospect.

Spiritual Underpinnings of Nature-Inspired Life and Living

The New Philosophy (TNP) published my essay, "The Spiritual Underpinnings of Nature Based Leadership" (January-June 2016). TNP is the journal of the Swedenborgian Scientific Association. I have since shifted my principal theme first to nature-inspired learning and leading. *Leadership* alone does not tell the whole story. And from there to nature-inspired life and living. I choose now to start at the roots, anchored in the fertile substrate of nature's wisdom, power, beauty, magic, wonder, and awe.

I drafted the TNP essay in mid-2015. I find no better roots for nature's inspiration and lessons than in a substrate that is deeply spiritual (or, in the case of the TNP article, Spiritual). I wrote in *Nature Based Leadership* of the absolute humility and inspiration I felt the first time I viewed Denali Mountain, North America's tallest peak, up close from nearby Mt. Quigley. Seldom do I witness and experience the wonder of nature without spiritual movement, spurring deep feelings in mind, heart, and soul. I cannot think of nature-inspired life and living without engaging Spirit.

Eighteenth century Swedish scientist, philosopher, and theologian Emanuel Swedenborg (1688-1772) adopted a central philosophical tenet, that the entire natural world comprises a series of physical symbols that correspond to a deeper spiritual reality. That is, nature embodies all lessons of life's physical and spiritual essence. Likewise, our natural world offers powerful truths applicable to living, learning, serving, and leading. I have found inspiration, solace, and illumination in the natural world, written more permanently, powerfully, and succinctly than any management text could possibly encapsulate.

Swedenborg believed that there is a perfect alignment between the spiritual and natural world, and that all observable *effects* in the natural world arise directly from correspondent *causes* in the spiritual world. Because of this spiritual reality, what often appears to be mere *coincidence*, when seen more deeply, can be regarded as *correspondence*.

I included six lessons from nature in the TNP essay. Not *the* six lessons. Just six examples. I employ one of those six lessons often in my speaking and teaching, the essential complementary forces of humility and inspiration. Developed fully in *Nature Based Leadership*, the lesson derives from when I summited Alaska's Mount Quigley (a rather insignificant peak twenty miles north of Denali), and realized I had a full view to the south. I stopped, turning my attention to that direction. My heart pounding, I saw only gleaming white with my level gaze. My eyes slowly following that white wall upward, my head tilting ever more toward the vertical, there stood the most magnificent sight of my life, before or since. McKinley rises 18,000 feet from the valley in front of me to its summit. Three and one-half vertical miles of rock, glaciers, and glory towered in the late morning sun.

Stunned, I felt two emotions. The first was total humility. In a few seconds I had gone from the arrogant satisfaction of "climbing" Quigley, to the full realization that I had done nothing. Competing, I felt absolute inspiration. I stood before The Mountain, grasping slowly what might be, what could be, what perhaps lies ahead. Inspiration to reach beyond my grasp; to celebrate every accomplishment but know that always more lies ahead.

A wise leader knows that humility is the place where inspiration happens:

> "When real humility is present in a person he surrenders all power to think or do anything by himself and abandons himself completely to the Divine, and in this condition draws near to the Divine."

Emanuel Swedenborg, AC 6866

> "The most ancient people were internal, and although they sensated the external things of the body and the world, they cared not for them; for in each object of sense they perceived something Divine and heavenly. For example, when they saw a high mountain, they perceived an idea, not of a mountain, but of elevation, and from elevation, of heaven and the Lord."

Emanuel Swedenborg, AC 920

As I revisited the TNP article, I am reminded how deeply intertwined are nature and my own spiritual journey. I'm pleased, too, that my own thinking has shifted from a focus on nature-based *leadership*, to nature-inspired *learning and leading*, to nature-inspired *life and living*. Applying nature's wisdom to life (and work) is central to my own approach to making tomorrow brighter, and to imploring that individuals and enterprises embrace our obligation to practice Earth stewardship. Only by adopting and practicing an Earth ethic can any society, and the individuals and enterprises composing it, truly ennoble the human race.

Sacred Places and Forest Cathedrals

I reflect from memory on those special places in nature that live within me, that left life-lasting impressions. We squirrel hunted on Martin's Mountain a few miles east of Cumberland, Maryland along U.S. Route 40, long before Interstate 68 eliminated the need to travel the winding National Road. Five decades have passed since last I entered those woods. I can recall vividly the hike from roadside: over the barbed-wire fence, a few hundred feet east through open woods, across an abandoned pasture reverting to cedar and hawthorn, among old orchard apple trees and scattered oak saplings. From there, I found open woods along an ephemeral stream, and then the fallen tree at the base of a steep north-facing hill where I sat, shotgun on my lap, awaiting the appearance of arboreal rodents.

I recall sitting, listening, watching: clouds racing (sometimes leisurely floating), leaves falling, acorns and hickory nuts dropping. Occasional deer meandering, searching the forest floor for acorns or simply heading somewhere else. The rare *raft* (the applicable collective noun) of turkeys scratching noisily, spooking and dispersing when they sensed me. Squirrels chattering and barking out of sight. Other times moving about in the canopy, scampering across the ground, feeding in the treetops, dropping hickory shell fragments as they gnawed the nuts. Once in a while, shooting and only sometimes connecting. The experience was much more about being there, inhaling deeply the fall magic. This cove hardwood site offered tall, straight boles and heavy crowns.

The early fall canopy cast deep shade that with the season's advance grew thin and eventually bare. At the season's start, I ascended to my spot with jacket tied at my waist; with November came extra layers, huddling from the wind while seated and shivering. I recall one late October watching and hearing sleet peppering me, my log seat, and the leaf-carpeted forest floor. I remember both wishing for a cooling breeze and six weeks later seeking shelter from a blasting gale whipping from the northwest. Mostly I remember the sense of peace, tranquility, and escape in being there in my private cathedral. I did not recognize at the time that this constituted the spiritual. I did not view it as anything beyond simply enjoying the outdoors.

Yet in my half-century rearview mirror, I long to be there to see it for what it was, a sacred place that transformed me and laid the groundwork for what I now am. Funny how when I think of my high school chums, I picture them as they were. I am shocked to see current photos on Facebook. They have changed as much as I. I am sure that my special place on Martin's Mountain has likewise morphed. Even were I to find the location where we parked, the forest and cover would show the mark of 50 years growth and stand dynamics. The abandoned pasture would be a closed and maturing forest. My fallen tree would be decayed rubble. Only the landform itself would be unchanged. I may want to revisit the site. However, I remind myself that so many things are richer in memory. I may just leave it there, stored along with other sacred places from across my life's journey.

Leopold concurred:

> "It is the part of wisdom never to revisit a wilderness, for the more golden the lily, the more certain that someone has gilded it."

I find it interesting that many of my sacred place memories come from my own experiences in nature that I faced alone, just me. I recently read Thoreau's *Walden*, struggling from time to time with style, language, and depth. He also spoke of his own appreciation of (no, insistence upon) solitude: "I find it wholesome to be alone the better part of the time. To be in company, even with the best, is soon wearisome and dissipating. I love to be alone. I never found the companion that was so companionable as solitude." My own relationship with nature grows more intense and spiritual when I experience nature in solitude.

Since retiring to northern Alabama, we visited Auburn where we lived from 1996-2001. We loved the forested neighborhood where we resided those five years. We viewed our nearly one-acre lot as sacred. As we entered the old neighborhood, drove past our house, and parked beyond it on a cul-de-sac, we began to see a major difference. Importantly, no additional construction had followed our leaving; all the lots had already been occupied by then. As we walked and gawked, the obvious dawned on me, a little slow on the uptake for an old forester. The Auburn area is blessed with an average annual temperature of 63 degrees and 53 inches of yearly rainfall. Growing seasons are long and rainfall plentiful throughout. Forests thrive, especially when they occupy well-tended, often fertilized and irrigated residential lots. What had been perhaps a 30-40 year-old-natural forest when we departed, now showed evidence of an additional 15 bountiful growing seasons. Open-growing, dominant oaks and pine had probably incremented up to an inch in diameter per growing season. A twelve-inch diameter tree when we left would now be two feet. Its crown would have expanded from large to massive. We saw tremendous difference in the landscape trees we had monitored and treasured during our five-year-stewardship.

The old neighborhood now gave the impression of houses in an old-growth forest. No wonder things seemed strange and unfamiliar. We recognized a few names on mailboxes, evidencing that some old neighbors along the street were still in residence. My guess is that they have little notion that things have changed. I say that for two reasons. First, annual changes are subtle and can easily escape notice. Secondly, most people are blind to the nuances and ways of nature. Only for the itinerant time travelers do the changes appear suddenly, and significantly. Judy and I—people who do pay attention, who do look and usually see—had to think our way to the obvious, suggesting that even we are at risk of occasionally not seeing. I admit some level of pique at myself; I should have anticipated that level of forest maturation.

We recalled another bit of time travel to a former residence. The company (Union Camp Corporation, for whom I worked from 1973-1985) moved us from southeastern Virginia to Savannah, Georgia in 1979. We returned to visit the old Virginia neighborhood 23 years later, driving up from our new post in the Raleigh, N.C. vicinity. When we bought our first home in 1974 in Sedley, Virginia, it occupied nearly an acre fronting a county road, the lot carved from a peanut field. We enjoyed a great garden and began planting loblolly pine seedlings in the front yard (east) as well as the north side (along and beyond our driveway). Our first home and lot in a marriage that has since carried 47 years, this was sacred ground, and our relationship to it fully and deeply spiritual. We departed to Savannah with those seedlings perhaps 5-7 feet tall. The yard still appeared to be an open lot with landscape plants. When we drove northward toward our old home, we were incredulous that it now stood in deep forest. Our pines (genetically improved Union Camp seedling stock, custom-selected and crossed for our region's soils and climate) towered 80 feet and provided full shade to the entire house and much of what had once been our young family's productive vegetable garden. Nothing is static!

I once sat dockside along Nova Scotia's Bay of Fundy, watching the incoming tide, at one point climbing the piers at nearly one inch per minute. It's hard to miss the flux, the tremendous surge, and rapid pace. Now, try sitting on your front porch to watch your oak tree grow. Walk inside to get a glass of Alabama "sweet tea," and return to the porch. Nothing will have changed. Instead, imagine walking inside, and then returning to the porch 15 years later. What moves only inexorably one minute, one hour, one year at a time, leaps, spurts, and bounds across a decade and a half.

The pace and scale of change remind me how fleeting is our individual time on Earth, and how limited is our window for making a difference. This morning I stopped at a place of business. I pulled into a parking spot beside a driver sitting, smoking, and absorbed in a digital device. After one final drag on the smoke, she tossed it out the window. Driving home, I stopped at a red light behind another smoker who took his own last draw, and likewise tossed the butt onto the road. Both incidents served as sad evidence that so few of us have a spiritual relationship to this sacred Earth. Pity our children, and theirs, and generations beyond unless we awaken to the cause of informed, dedicated, and responsible stewardship. Callous disregard for this Earth and our future will not serve us well. I want to spread my core message of nature-inspired life and living. Yet I struggle with how we reach our digital- and nicotine-addicted fellow Earth residents.

Hyrum Smith captured the essence of our plight beautifully and compellingly:

> "I began to recognize that there are powers out there
> that are much greater than you. There are forces out
> there – natural laws, if you will. And if you don't make

the conscious decision to live by those laws, there are going to be painful consequences."

Some 500 years ago, Leonardo da Vinci distilled our existence to its fundamental truths. One of nature's causes is to self-renew, to assure that one generation succeeds another, and that life prevails deeply into the future:

> "Nature is full of infinite causes that have never occurred in experience."

Leonardo da Vinci, *Favorite Report*

And yet I worry deeply that we will never reach (nor teach) enough of our fellow Earth travelers to make a difference. The core of our plight and the depth of our responsibility stay hidden from view. Too many of us are blind to our peril. I am dedicating my remaining years to the cause. Wendell Berry lived and wrote of cause. His prose is poetry; his words lyrics; his message both power and spirit:

> "When despair for the world grows in me and I wake in the night at the least sound in fear of what my life and my children's lives may be, I go and lie down where the wood drake rests in his beauty on the water, and the great heron feeds. I come into the peace of wild things who do not tax their lives with forethought of grief. I come into the presence of still water. And I feel above me the day-blind stars waiting with their light. For a time, I rest in the grace of the world, and am free."

Occasionally I want to retreat to one of my own sacred places, to "come into the peace of wild things who do not tax their lives with forethought of grief." I want to rest "in the grace of the world." The spirit of the land anchors me, guides me, and inspires me. When I am one with nature, in sacred embrace of it, I am free. Nature is my daily bread. Nature's lifeblood courses through my veins, and will so long as there is life within me.

Being A Spiritual Ecologist

JJW

The term **spiritual ecology** is most simply used to refer
to the spiritual dimension of our present ecological
crisis. Practitioners within and outside of academia,
conservation, and religion recognize—and have begun
to create a body of work that supports—this idea.

There is a divine spark—an inexplicable and awesome miracle in
which spirit and matter converge—in every tree and lake; robin and
rabbit; estuary and glacier; microbe, beetle, butterfly, krill; grain of sand
and spawning salmon. This sacredness is in Earth. And it is the same
holiness each one of us carries within. It connects us for better and for
worse. When the Earth and her inhabitants are hurt or destroyed, so
too are we. When the soul of this planet is crying for healing, so too
is ours. The Earth reflects *our* being, and we mirror *it* as well. As the
environment becomes fragmented, more species become extinct, the
crisis requires us to move back into participation with this sacred aspect
of being—our own and the Earth's.

Recognizing that we are in union with the natural world, and
actively working to reunite with it, *is* a spiritual calling.

The natural world has always been a place of healing and restoration
for me. As a young girl growing up in a very urban environment of

cement sidewalks, paved streets, asphalt "blacktops" at school, and modern vehicles and conveniences of all sorts, the word "nature" took on an almost otherworldly shimmer. Every ornamental, cultivated species (which composed the majority of plants in the gardens in the small yards of my hometown) was "nature" and belonged there; I didn't have concepts for things like non-native species, or words like "endemic" in my vocabulary until two decades later. I loved them all. I bemoaned the chores that included eradicating something growing from something not-growing, like the weeds sprouting up in the earthquake-cracked cement driveway. My six-year-old self "rooted" for those green gifts and was frustrated trying to tease out adults' notion of "weed" from "desirable," "cultivated." Any grassy lawn, flower or bush, walnut, crow, or snail—however isolated from the thriving ecosystem of interspecies relationships and physical features of which it might once have been a native—was definable to me as "nature." Not only were *they* nature, I knew that I was—inexplicably—*part of* it all.

Bare Essence

Though "spiritual ecology" is a term in its infancy, the beliefs and values it espouses are ancient; Earth-based cultures and eco-spiritualities have long considered respect for nature as central to all endeavors. Moreover, the sacred nature of ecology and humans' innate sanctity as members of the community of all living beings are primal; it is our forgotten recognition of this which is at the heart of spiritual ecology. At its very center, spiritual ecology acknowledges the dire crisis in which we now find ourselves in regard to the degradation of Earth. It also recognizes our role in it—species loss, climate change, ecosystem fragmentation, pollution (air, water, noise) ... The link between values and practices that see the *inherent sacred in nature* and, simultaneously, our responsibility toward the Earth expressed as *spiritual responses and attitudes* (in addition to physical ones) is paramount to spiritual ecologists. There are many notable conservationists and environmentalists, wilderness guides, therapists, clergy (from many religions and faith traditions), activists, writers, and others, whose life work is considered part of this interdisciplinary body we call "spiritual ecology." Among them are: Thomas Berry, Joanna Macy, Llewellyn Vaughan-Lee, Bill Plotkin, Vandana Shiva, Wendell Berry, Thich Nhat Hanh. I would be sorely remiss if I didn't admit that this is only a very partial list. Not all of these people would claim the label "spiritual ecologist" but their life's work is squarely at the center of these ideas and practices.

Now, I am a spiritual ecologist. I always have been, though my embrace of this term as a professional identity is coincident with the fairly recent formal acknowledgment of the ideas undergirding spiritual ecology as an interdisciplinary philosophy with practical application. That is, my own longtime, multidisciplinary work in environmental studies, creativity, spirituality, and research found a home in the newly-emergent field of spiritual ecology.

Public Claiming

In 2015, I was deeply honored that my proposal to present my work at the Parliament of the World's Religions was accepted. This recurrent global interfaith gathering is attended by ten thousand people from more than eighty nations and representing over fifty faiths. This was the first major exposure my work had to a truly interfaith experience. My heart sang from the moment I arrived at the Parliament presentation venue. I was scarcely aware that I was in the city's convention center as soon as I reached the near curb. I was greeted by colorful banners, sacred objects, photos, clothing, and adornments of all sorts on people of all faiths, ethnicities, races; books, holy texts, pamphlets, quotations; holy fires, sacred sand mandalas, an indoor labyrinth; rooms converted into sanctuaries with icons, candles, incense, bells, crosses, holy water, cloths, ribbons, scarves, engravings, sculptures; quiet rooms, meditation spaces, altars, prayer rooms … all from a myriad of religions and faith-based traditions. In the main meeting space where plenary speakers and moderators took the stage at a number of podiums—foreground to the several theater-sized projection screens and behind the dozens of television monitors throughout the great hall—thousands of people were seated and standing at various points during the several-days-long Parliament. There was a huge area in another part of the building that contained hundreds of booths and tables filled with information, books, couches and chairs, beautiful images from multifarious faiths, indoor forests, Internet stations. Everywhere people were smiling or in deep discussion. Nearly everyone I met offered a hug in greeting, in lieu of the standard handshake or bow of most cultures.

All ten-thousand-odd-of-us were given a delicious, free lunch offered by the Sikh community; many Sikhs had traveled from across the globe to be of service preparing, serving, and cleaning up. Thousands of us removed our shoes, covered our heads with a scarf, and sat on beautiful carpets laid over the cold cement floor while men and women of the Sikh faith came around with metal buckets to ladle generous portions of sumptuous lentils, beans, rice, and vegetables onto our plates. This experience, repeated every day of the Parliament, was one of the highlights of generosity and interfaith communion.

Each morning just after dawn, attendees had an opportunity to learn about various faith traditions from adherents, clergy, or elders, through attendance at a religious observance in the tradition of the religion or spiritual practice. The underlying idea of this interfaith gathering is to find common ground and to learn from one another. It is not a space in which proselytizing is accepted; it *is* a space in which justice, tolerance, peace, and compassion are driving forces. It is not divisive; it is unifying. I was truly transformed by this experience. Not converted, but *transformed*: to see how thousands of people with deeply-held religious convictions could come together in the true spirit of humanity and divinity was a first for me.

My workshop was well-attended by people of many faiths; not a single person in the room called themselves a spiritual ecologist—except for me. Yet each one of them listened to my presentation and heartily engaged the creative, nature-based practices that have become the inspired cornerstone of my professional work. I asked the participants to experience their own traditions—denying nothing of their deeply-held beliefs—as they moved through the activities I offered. By the end of our time together, the attendees had crafted new ways to incorporate the practices I presented into a cohesive Earth-revering addition to their own faith rituals. An opening of all of our hearts toward our broader, innate divinity as humans-inseparable-from-Earth became manifest that day.

Declaring myself a "spiritual ecologist," claiming it for the first time publicly as I traveled to and met people at the Parliament, was an affirming experience. I do not have a church, hall, temple, synagogue, or other place of worship to attend that espouses and practices "spiritual ecology." Because it is a multidisciplinary set of ideas, composed of people from many religious and faith traditions—and of none—a practice of spiritual ecology can be isolating. It is not a religion or a faith tradition, as such. But it undergirds and underscores the deep sanctity of our interrelationship with the natural world, and with all beings (including humans). For me, being a spiritual ecologist is much richer than merely holding to (agreeing with) the set of values and beliefs at its core, and is much broader than a single religious doctrine. Spiritual ecologists come in the shape of Buddhists, Christians, Hindus, believers in undefined broad spiritual practice, Sufi mystics, Earth-based religious practitioners, and more.

Spiritual Journey to Spiritual Ecology

From my earliest years, I began connecting nature to spirituality in addition to wellbeing. The occasional church camps that I attended for a week at a time were held at a conference center several winding hours' drive away, up in the mountains at a place loaded with ponderosa pine trees. The warm air heating the bark created a scent that is unforgettable for me; even as an adult, smelling the warmed sap of a ponderosa pine invokes something holy in me. I do not need to live in the ponderosa pine woods; but I do need to remember their significance in my growing up years as a place of sacred retreat. These particular church camps for children were fairly standard: prayers before meals, a Bible lesson or two during the day, a campfire at night, a host of outdoor activities and nature-based crafts, and lots of singing (children's songs about Jesus and God, and even "Father Abraham"). In fourth grade I said "the sinner's prayer" so that I could become "saved." I was even interviewed on the local Christian radio station about my conversion experience at the fourth grade Bible camp. My relationship to this church deepened, as did my faith, as I entered high school. By ninth grade, I was being baptized a second time (the first was in sixth grade by the pastor in the church baptismal)—my youth group leader baptized me in the Pacific Ocean. And then I was fully immersed: my entire social life and spiritual life centered around the youth group, weekly Bible studies, Sunday church (and later I taught Children's Church), and retreats.

Our high school group was small but very committed to our faith; we opted to have regular fasting retreats up in the same ponderosa pines forest as the church camps of my childhood. We generally left on a Friday after school and returned Sunday late afternoon; we would drink only water or juice between lunch on Friday and breakfast on Sunday. And for the day-and-a-half fast we would spread out on the property—most people in the cabin, a few of us outside—and pray. Literally, I would pray and pray and pray for hours. Most of the time I found a totally isolated spot with a tree trunk to sit against. I would look up at the tall pines and imagine God was up there just above the topmost needles that swept the very heavens, it seemed. I would place my hands down on the pine-needle blanket I sat on and feel bits of sap staining my hands. I would raise those sticky palms in clasped prayer and make my beseechings on behalf of others. All the while the sweet, pine-scented breeze would blow through my long hair, and my eyes were filled with visions of holy trees on heavenly mountains. It was pure reverie, bliss, sacred time. (I also recall the nearly-nauseating let down at the end of the weekends when our buoyant spirits returned home to the secular world of responsibility, ordinary routines, concrete lives in right angles, troubles.)

Those times on the mountain were genuine and sacred for me. They stood in sharp contrast to everyday profane life. And the peaks and pines themselves became not just the *site* for holy conversion but the actual symbol—and later, *embodiment*—of all that is divinely spiritual for me. I left the church of my youth and searched for the sacred in other places. But over the years, I continued to have moments in nature that spoke deeply to me, that were actual "spiritual experiences."

It is no wonder to me that decades later, in one of my roughest patches in life, I turned to the most intense form of spiritual seeking in the natural world: vision quests. I had already deeply studied various religious traditions and attended myriad holy services and observances with friends from different faiths. From that insightful journey I developed personal spiritual practices embracing an interfaith expression of spirituality. Sweat lodges; Buddhist meditation; Earth-based spiritual rituals; visits to synagogues, mosques, temples, sanctuaries, chapels, churches, monasteries, meeting houses, shrines, cathedrals; and other religious and spiritual diversity informed and inspired my spiritual practices. But during the midlife time of crisis, I woke up one day (having friends who had amply shared about their wilderness guiding work) and said to myself, "I cannot *not* do a vision quest." And waves of fear swept over me: I knew nothing about fasting for four days and four nights, being out in the wilderness alone with no shelter, and I certainly did not think it would be enjoyable nor, probably, revelatory. But the conviction that I must do a wilderness rite of passage would not leave me. I tried to deny it … or to rationalize it away. I didn't speak it aloud to anyone for months. I privately engaged every fear I had about it until they were cougar-sized imaginal nightmares. But nearly every day I heard it again: *cannot* not *do it.*

While this chapter does not lend itself to the whole story of that eventual vision quest, nor to the several wilderness fasts I did in the following years, I mention it here as a segue to the theme I present next: that nature—particularly untouched wilderness—is a mirror for the soul. My deepest insights about life, my most painful turning points or transitions, and the most revelatory and celebratory moments of my life are all wrapped up in the natural world: its beauty and agonies, its teachings and lessons, its cycles and inspirations. The natural world in all of its tangible manifestations (trees, the ocean, weather, seasons, moonrises and sunsets, coyotes, rabbits, wasps) and all of its symbolism (totems, metaphors, burning bushes, and the like) is fodder for human understanding about our life. The natural world can bathe us in the vivid arc of a rainbow or the sweet autumn rain. And as it does so we can learn something about ourselves, our relationship to the divine, and our deeper purpose in the world. The Earth offers us the sacred and the profane; we can use both to deepen our experience of daily life.

But this does not happen unless we are engaged in the natural world. I mean: unless we are *out there* in it. A person does not have to do the extreme wilderness rite of passage of a several-day vision quest in order to move deeper or forward into life. We *do* need to put our hands in the warm summer soil, take time to savor the spring birdsong, pause in the deep silence of a winter snowfall, slowly inhale the musky scent of late autumn. We need to recognize and accept that some creatures are less seemly to us (*Rodentia?*) while others charm us into broad smiles (pandas?). Without courageously peering into these extremes that live within us, and without making the journey to the center of our polarized ascriptions between "good" or "likeable" and "bad" or "unlovable," we will have difficulty moving to the balanced center of a spiritual life or the glorious and gory life that is nature.

My experiences in nature led to passion, which led to sanctity.

Life as a Spiritual Ecologist

I have very distinct practices, and things I avoid doing, that encompass and encapsulate my work and lifestyle as a spiritual ecologist. Morals; rituals, ceremonies, and holidays; physical, emotional, mental, and spiritual wellbeing; and mortality are the aspects of my life that best illustrate and embody my values and practices of being a spiritual ecologist. These are *my* orientation to spiritual ecology, and any departure from the body of work and practice that is formally recognized as "spiritual ecology" is reflective of my own nuances; my personal perspective is not intended to be in argument or conflict with the field.

Morals

The definition at the top of this chapter links "ecological crisis" with "spiritual dimension." Not every environmentalist is an adherent to a religion, and not every spiritual or religious person cares about and for Earth and nonhuman beings. But the recognition of the divine in nature is a call to behave from our deepest, or biggest, or most sacred selves as we navigate ways to address the myriad environmental concerns that, together, place us at a major turning point in regard to the health of the very planet that supports us. It is a recognition, also, of the divine in us (as we *are* part of the beautiful web of nature, though we are apt to forget or deny that actuality when it suits us). Nature is sacred; we are sacred. My personal sense of right and wrong, the guide to navigating my principles from day to day, is rooted in my understanding that my actions impact other humans as well as the Earth and all nonhuman beings.

This is one of the greatest gifts, I believe, of being a spiritual ecologist: I am naturally inclined toward a meaningful spiritual life and I am totally in love with the natural world. I do believe we have a responsibility to care for this planet and her beings. I also know we need one another, and a deep caring for other humans is as central to my personal expression of being a spiritual ecologist as is my deep caring for Earth. I recently published a book about writing and nature—how they are intertwined and in dynamic interaction with one another—and throughout the text I repeat the idea that we humans are inextricably intertwined, or interconnected, with nature. Striving for a "right relationship" with nature is predicated on behaving respectfully toward nature ("right actions"). Many of these "right actions" can be found in the great religions; simply open a holy text near you and notice the references to nature. And I believe the way to right actions toward the environment begins with reacquainting ourselves with the flora, fauna, skies and seas, and the landscapes around us. Getting familiar with all that lives, breathes, and moves in the out of doors. Further, I believe these right actions, this familiarity, a right relationship, begin with each individual, in fact with*in* each individual. So, this is the professional work I do on a daily basis: guiding individuals through their inner/outer landscapes—through their inner worlds and the outer physical world (especially that which is not human-made)—in order that they may deepen their relationship with themselves and with nature (which are one), becoming whole and becoming balanced.

For me, a right relationship with nature is inclusive of humans' wellbeing; I am interested in human social issues, peace-building, civility, kindness, compassion. Over the past several years, I have gotten more formally involved in the kindness, gratitude, and compassion movements (including Random Acts, A Network for Grateful Living, and Charter for Compassion). My work has included webinars and courses, blog posts, interviews, essays that help people move more deeply into right relationship with themselves, with other humans, and with the natural world. For more than forty-two years, I have also been continuously engaged as a volunteer in community service work of many different sorts: environmental activism, conservation work, crisis clinics, hospitals and nursing homes, food banks and shelters; and for the past nearly-twenty years, I have focused my volunteerism on hospice, grief and loss, bereavement issues. Sitting at the bedsides of people who are dying and supporting their loved ones have been the most gratifying contributions I have made to the wellbeing of humans. I have incorporated my passion and work in the natural world into my hospice service in many ways, and then written about it and trained other volunteers so that they can do so also.

All of this is not to place undue focus on humans. My understanding and practice of spiritual ecology—and the morality and resulting behaviors I am thus inclined to do—are, first and foremost, rooted in the natural world. I have spent decades informally and formally learning about, researching, writing about, conserving, spending time in, and focusing my daily actions on how I (as an individual) and humanity (all of our lives together) can behave more responsibly in regard to Earth's precious—and finite—natural resources. And when I write "responsibly," I also mean "kindly, lovingly, in balance with" other creatures and the biotic environment with which we are intertwined. Most of what this all boils down to for me (including the decades of scholarly pursuit) is living day to day in a way that does little harm to nature and her beings, is minimally consumptive of natural resources, and honors the cycles and miracles that are daily expressed by and in the natural world.

A sunrise.

Birds hatching.

Fiery autumn leaves.

Tides.

Other moral considerations that are part of my practice as a spiritual ecologist involve paying attention to my "footprint"—the size of my living space; reuse and waste; whether or not I drive a vehicle and, if so, its carbon emissions; energy and water use. I like to be mindful of the small everyday things as well: the type of wrapping I use on a gift, the amount of food on my plate, the materials from which a purchased item are constructed. Many of my major life decisions have also followed from consideration of the natural environment and resources: whether or not to own a house, or bear children, or have lots of possessions. In any given moment, these are not easy or simple choices. How, for example, I have chosen to handle a mouse or wasp infestation in my home has varied over time and on my condition in the moment; just because I *can* use a lethal mouse trap or insecticide doesn't necessarily mean I *should*. It is not about being perfectly aligned with all beings in any given moment; it *is* about being thoughtful each time I am faced with a situation that involves another creature—pest or not.

Rituals, Ceremonies, and Holidays

I have chosen not to participate in major American holidays for much of my adult life. Again, these were not always easy or clear-cut decisions. During the years I was partnered with a man whose family was very traditional, I participated at the minimally-acceptable level in a material sense yet strived to participate cheerfully and helpfully. I have opted to add solstices and equinoxes to my calendar, to honor and mark the seasons. Sometimes this has taken the shape of a nature sculpture or outdoor creative endeavor on the particular day noted as the season change. I have sometimes conducted an impromptu ceremony to mark natural disasters: the earthquake that broke many precious artifacts, several major appliances, and virtually all of my dishes; the fires that raged in neighboring states and created clouds of ash and haze that hung over my home for weeks; the flood that took the lives of many; a volcano I have never seen that claimed the homes and lives—and lakes and forests—of a land far from me; and the drought that continues to plague particular areas not far from where I grew up. The things I do to mark or honor, celebrate or mourn, do not always take the shape of beauty offerings; sometimes I write a blog post, journal, engage in service work in memory of what was, what happened, and what is now. The other day I found a beautiful sparrow lying dead in my yard, and my choice to carry it to the edge of the field and bury it, to offer a few kind words about its life, and to decorate the burial spot with just-fallen flowers from my garden was an instinctive and immediate act, a spontaneous celebration and honoring of what I encountered as I roamed through my grass. Then I wrote about it as a way of further giving attention to something that may well have gone unnoticed. I have done this type of thing my entire life.

We can move closer to a spirituality of full compassion, a complete embrace of even those creatures we have been taught to fear or dislike, *by direct experience* of our own varying relationships to particular species.

Physical, Emotional, Mental, and Spiritual Wellbeing

As a spiritual ecologist, my entire being is engaged in the relationship with nature. It is not just a practice of spirituality or environmental concern. I also need to involve the physical, emotional, and mental aspects of my life in the nature-based practices and convictions. Walking, hiking, visiting new landscapes and natural areas are ways I get my body involved in the process of spiritual ecology. Movement (particularly in nature) was something that I relied on as a practice for wellbeing since my earliest years. As a little girl, I didn't realize that roller skating, walking to and from school, bicycling, playing in the green spaces and treed areas near my home were ways to feel better physically, but in retrospect it is so clear to me that it was not an option, but rather an imperative, that I do so; without these long stretches of movement, I would have wilted.

The inner renewal and sustenance that benefit, soothe, and heal my emotional landscape when I have spent time out of doors, particularly in natural areas (forests, beaches, meadows, mountains…), are invaluable to who I am and how I am in the built world of humans. Meditation and prayer, sitting in silence, walking a labyrinth, are actual "activities" I can engage in nature to help make the connection between nature's healing balm and the wounded places within. Though after decades of time in the natural world in many different places and ecosystems, I can easily trace the emotional wellbeing I felt in such places by viewing a photograph, engaging in a reverie about a natural area, or recalling a story of such an experience. That is, it is embedded in me now.

Even my mind, the ability to think and learn and discern, has been aided throughout my life by nature. I might today study a new pattern of bird movement in my yard, or research the nestling phase of a particular avian, by spending time in nature. I want to learn about the world outside my door, to understand the cycles and habits of seasons and creatures. Recently I attended a book reading at our lovely local bookstore; the author had written a tome about tides based on travels and study all over the world. I was enthralled with his talk and intrigued by what I learned; I was also stunned by how little I actually did know about tides, especially after living on islands in tidal waters for so many of my adult years. Not only is learning about nature a crucial aspect of who I am and how I view my work as a spiritual ecologist (learning about various aspects of the climate change crisis we are in, for example), it is also the beneficiary of my time in nature. That is, I have gained a wealth of insights and inspiration (the latter as much a part of my spiritual life as my intellectual one) from spending time in nature. Some years ago, during a professional transition, I needed to reconceptualize what I was doing and how I presented that to the world. For several months, I spent every day working on a particular project. I would give it everything I had in the morning and then when I reached an impasse (about how to proceed), I would take my dog to a local natural area and hike around, paying attention to the weather and creatures, the light and textures. I would empty my mind as I strode deeper into the natural area. And then it would happen, every single day: I would suddenly have an idea, insight, or a clear next step about my work project. I would write it all down when I got back in the car or had arrived home. And then I would incorporate that information into the project. Just like this, it all got fleshed out until I had a completed project and a clear articulation of my work.

Though I've already discussed some aspects of my spiritual practices in regard to spiritual ecology, I want to add one more quick note.

Inspiration and faith, for me, are directly linked back to how I engage in the natural world around me. In moments when things have been difficult, or I've struggled to find hope in a despairing situation, the blessing of a breeze, a coyote passing through the yard, the call of an owl, or the wafting scent of cherry blossom has arrived to save me, to renew my faith, to restore my sense of wellbeing. And most of all, to connect me back to something larger and more enduring than myself: divine nature.

Mortality

Spiritual ecology even stretches into how I view mortality—my own and others'. In my state, we have a legal end of life document called the Five Wishes. In this small, several-page form, there are deeply personal questions about how a person wants to spend their final days. Different from a power of attorney or do not resuscitate order, the Five Wishes asks the completer of the form to give detailed information about comfort, treatment by others, and information that the person wants loved ones to know. There are places on the form where things can be simply crossed out if they are not desirable. And places where things we do want can be added. I was talking with a dear friend about this document recently; I mentioned how vitally important it is to me to have the sights, sounds, scents, tastes, and touch of nature all around me in my final hours. A window full of warm sun or a cool breeze, a moonrise, and flowers, birdsong and rain and a fresh strawberry on my lips. I want my corpus to be environmentally reduced and my ashes spread: the final act of deep reintegration with the natural world.

I also incorporate a lot of objects from and images of nature in my volunteer service work. Recently I have begun to share these ideas with professionals in the hospice and palliative care field through articles I've written and in-services I've provided. When I am assigned to be the volunteer for a person who is dying, it is not uncommon for me to find pleasing and soothing ways to bring nature into my time with that person as well as with their family. Practices as simple as offering a bouquet of wildflowers I picked, a photograph I've taken of a flower, or end of life review that incorporates the person's important interactions with various landscapes or natural features in their lifetime are common ways I bring this into my service work. Of course, if I am able to help someone who wants to get outside to do so, this is another simple way of connecting them back to nature. For people who are bedbound, I often bring nature objects into the room, or remind them what season it is and what the weather feels like outside. Many times, I have offered the opportunity for caregivers and family members to get outside (for a walk, gardening, time to sit quietly…) while I am there with their loved one.

For me, being a spiritual ecologist is a full embrace of body, emotion, mind, and spirit and reaches into every facet of my life.

The Deepest Essence

The brevity of and overly-simplistic personal examples in this chapter are intended to illustrate some means to an everyday practice of spiritual ecology. But they should not be taken as the sum total of it; the crucial significance at the root of spiritual ecology is humans' amnesia about the inner sacred and the divine inherent in the natural world. These are paramount to a true understanding of spiritual ecology. That is, it is not enough to have daily practices or even to recognize the divine in some aspects of the natural world. It is a fusing of both: a reintegration of a sanctity that is at once encompassing of human nature and nonhuman nature in balance, whole, freed from the deception and illusion of separability … and … a reverence for the sacred that is transcendent and full of awe. We are out of balance with ourselves, and with humanity. We are no longer whole, nor is the Earth. We are beyond an environmental crisis; we are at a *sacred* crisis: material concerns have largely replaced spiritual depth. Our vision is narrow, short-term, and ripped from the fabric of our true nature: seamless unity with Earth.

If we are to strive toward the deepest well-being and health, we can rely on an integrated spiritual ecological focus to move us there. We can do so by finding our appropriate balance in the broader world (human *and* nonhuman); becoming aware of the ways in which we have lost touch with divine nature; as well as nurturing a powerful, personal, integrated spiritual path that is respectfully inclusive of biotic and ecological life as well as the body of humanity. We can do so by exploring all the ways in which we are alienated from parts of ourselves (experiences, perspectives, illnesses of emotional and spiritual origin, etc.): our deepest inner work. We can do so by engaging in the collective work of healing and reintegration with others and Earth. We can do so by feeling our own pain, then other humans' agonies, then—ultimately— the anguish of a broken Earth.

As I type the ending to this chapter, my eyes glance out at the white world of an unusually-severe Pacific Northwest winter snowstorm; the authorities have declared a "state of emergency." But what I see are Douglas fir branches heavy with the thick white powder and the alder branches obscured by a frozen wet icing. Cascades of layered snow are being knocked free by an unseen breeze sending micro-showers of snowflakes tumbling in odd piles. Though I usually crave color, the sight is stunningly beautiful. Our electricity (heat, water, light) has just been cut off by a power wire that was loosened by the weight of the snow, landing askew on a treetop that then caught fire. So, it is silent here. Monochrome white. Nearly nightfall. All day I have felt as if I'm in a snow globe, massive swirls of milky flakes dominating my view. I am just one human in the entirety of the unified ecological web. I pray for those who have no shelter tonight … wherever in the world they are, whoever in the world they are. I send out cries for peace and safety. My own recent losses cycle back around to consciousness and I hold my breath as a wave of grief washes over; then I breathe it in, exhale it out. I recall the deer tracks in the blanket of snow and remember that her demise is mine. I am in awe: overwhelmed by reverence for cycles and seasons, vibrance and decay, and the potent and diverse family of Earth which I am privileged to enjoy this day, this moment. Spiritual ecology is a message of unity, beholding glory, compassion (*feeling with*), service. It is a recognition of the divinity that we share with the very holy planet that sustains us, and a call to respond to the needs of the world—to its *very* healing—with our hearts fully bathed in prayer.

Conclusion

John Muir wrote 130 years ago, "When we contemplate the whole globe as one great dewdrop, striped and dotted with continents and islands, flying through space with other stars all singing and shining together as one, the whole universe appears as an infinite storm of beauty." I see that infinite storm of beauty wherever I wander, a fact evident in each of my *Weaned Seals and Snowy Summits* essays.

I co-authored this book with recognition that humanity's future depends on fellow citizens appreciating this Earth we call home and accepting our individual and collective obligation to embrace and practice Earth stewardship. During my drafting, sparked by the cause driving me, I developed for the first time in my life a personal mission and vision. Mission: Employ writing and speaking to educate, inspire, and enable readers and listeners to understand, appreciate, and enjoy nature. Vision: People of all ages will pay greater attention *to* and engage more regularly *with* nature, and will accept and practice informed and responsible Earth stewardship. They will see their relationship to our natural world with new eyes and will understand more clearly their Earth home.

Dr. Wilhoit shares the drive to leave our Earth a better place and to ensure a brighter tomorrow for this pale blue orb. We chose the format of alternating chapters addressing similar themes to emphasize that two individuals with different life experiences and perspectives can commit to common purpose. We don't always agree on specific elements of practice and philosophy, yet we share a desired future condition outcome. We believe our differences enrich our joint book.

Interestingly, we have never met face-to-face, unless we count video-conferencing. I particularly value my co-author's flare for the art of Earth stewardship and her more poetic view of the human relationship to nature at both local and global levels. I believe my own view is directed more toward the science of Earth-care, also from local to global.

I shall remain forever grateful for Dr. Wilhoit's editing. She repeatedly rescued me from myself regarding formatting, punctuation, italicizing, and other nuances of writing that I may never master.

Perhaps most importantly, we quite easily agreed upon and enthusiastically embraced a working subtitle for our book and stayed with it to the end: *Stories of Passion for Place and Everyday Nature.* I recall the old saw, "People don't care how much you know until they know how much you care." We care deeply. We enjoyed collaborating and grew immensely from it.

As I write and speak about nature-inspired life and living, I learn that many who preceded me stated far better than I certain truths that I felt I might have been the first to discover. In that regard, like so much else in life, I again and again taste humility. Concomitantly, I derive inspiration from discovering that my thinking, retrospectively, finds resonance with long-gone giants in the field, Leopold, Muir, Thoreau, and Da Vinci among them.

I hope that Dr. Wilhoit and I have opened a doorway similar to what Muir saw in nature, "Between every two pines is a doorway to a new world." ...*SBJ*

On Earth Day 2019—just a week ago—I helped as family and friends closed out the affairs on a just-over-three-acres property on a neighboring island. A pearl of land with meadows, a stream, and edged by the mixed conifer/deciduous forest native to the Pacific Northwest, this parcel had been home to my mother for the last ten years of her life.

We awoke to the heartbreaking loveliness of wrens, robins, and black-capped chickadees singing the dawn into being. Relief and sadness alternated throughout the day as we packed, stored, or disseminated the remainder of the material possessions of a life well-lived. The rain that had been pervasive over recent weeks had abated and striking sunbreaks punctuated the day, highlighting the fluorescent green of new spring leaves. The three resident deer that my two sisters and I had come to call "the sisters" were nibbling on the blackberry leaves on the far side of the front grass. The willow that my mother loved, non-native to Western Washington but commonly planted for its sheltering beauty, cascaded down in boughs heavy with vernal growth.

I paused repeatedly on that day to drink in the nourishing sights and sounds of these beings who shared the land with my mom. They represent the same species that inhabit the nearby island on which I live, though these particular individuals were the very ones my mother had enjoyed and the very ones who will remain on that property. It is not an overstatement to mention that my connection with these avian, floral, and faunal inhabitants—both on my mom's property as well as around my own home—has been a deeply healing one. In recent months, but also over the course of my entire life, nature has sustained me physically, emotionally, mentally, and spiritually. I will likely never again experience an Earth Day that is so strikingly memorable.

We have sought, as we share with you in this book our personal stories (such as this one) and our professional stories (such as those detailing our work on behalf of the planet), to demonstrate how we are intertwined as humans and nonhumans on this Earth. We have strived to detail the myriad ways in which we can connect with both the awe-inspiring and everyday expressions of nature. We have dared to hope that our stories are thought-provoking, inspiring, and indicative of our deep passion for Earth in all of her manifestations. We have also challenged ourselves and each other to write a unified message from our diverse and unique backgrounds and perspectives.

This book has been an incredible learning experience for us. And, as Steve mentioned, we have thoroughly enjoyed it. I'm so grateful to be on the planet with like-hearted others who share in the glory and work of making explicit and tangible our deep reverence for and utter interdependence with all of the growing and crawling, flying and swimming ones. As Thich Nhat Hanh encourages, may you find within yourself that shining gem of compassion for all that live and breathe:

> "Waking up this morning, I smile, twenty-four brand new hours are before me. I vow to live fully in each moment and to look at all beings with eyes of compassion."

And may you honor your own self, the very Earth from which we are created:

> "How wonderful to be who I am, made out of Earth and water."
>
> Mary Oliver

Finally, may you reunite with all that is wild within and outside of you. ...JJW

About the Authors

Jennifer J. Wilhoit, Ph.D. is a published author, spiritual ecologist, and the founder of *TEALarbor stories*. She compassionately supports people's creative and healing processes by drawing from nature's wisdom. Jennifer works as a consultant, peacemaker, healer, and writer; she is also a longtime hospice, sacred vigiling, and bereavement volunteer. In addition to her individual practice with clients, Jennifer offers presentations, workshops, courses, trainings, and retreats. Her books, articles, and blogs focus on the human/nature relationship—what she calls "the inner/outer landscape." Jennifer is a faculty member and partner of the Charter for Compassion's Education Institute; an active board member of several environmental, peacebuilding, compassion-focused, and interfaith organizations; and has presented her work at the widely-attended, international Parliament of the World's Religions. When she is not researching, writing or working, Jennifer hikes, makes beauty in and photographs natural landscapes; reads; travels (internationally, as often as possible); and dabbles in creative arts. Jennifer thrives in the beautiful Pacific Northwest landscape where she lives. Learn more: **www.tealarborstories.com**

Steve Jones holds a bachelor's degree in forestry and a Ph.D. in applied ecology. Following his forestry degree, he dedicated 12 years to practicing his craft with a Fortune 500 Paper and Allied Products Manufacturing company in the six southeastern states from Virginia through Alabama. He returned to SUNY College of Environmental Science and Forestry to earn his doctoral degree. He has since held positions at nine universities, reporting directly to the CEO at three and serving as CEO at four. He claims to be a naïve forester who stumbled into higher education administration! Across his career he and his wife Judy (since June 1972) have made thirteen interstate moves, including to and from Alaska. Retired since January 2018, Steve considers himself a lifelong nature enthusiast, environmental educator, Earth steward, author, speaker, land ethicist, husband, father, and grandfather. Steve's written Mission Statement is to: Employ writing and speaking to educate, inspire, and enable readers and listeners to understand, appreciate, and enjoy Nature … and accept and practice Earth stewardship. Learn more: **stevejonesgbh.com**